ALSO BY PAUL HOFMANN

The Sunny Side of the Alps:
Year-Round Delights in South Tyrol and the Dolomites

The Spell of the Vienna Woods:
Inspiration and Influence from Beethoven to Kafka

Roma: The Smart Traveler's Guide to the Eternal City

That Fine Italian Hand

Cento Città: A Guide to the "Hundred Cities & Towns" of Italy

The Viennese: Splendor, Twilight, and Exile

O Vatican! A Slightly Wicked View of the Holy See

Rome: The Sweet, Tempestuous Life

The Seasons of Rome: A Journal

Switzerland: The Smart Traveler's Guide to Zurich, Basel, and Geneva

Umbria

⌣∴⌣

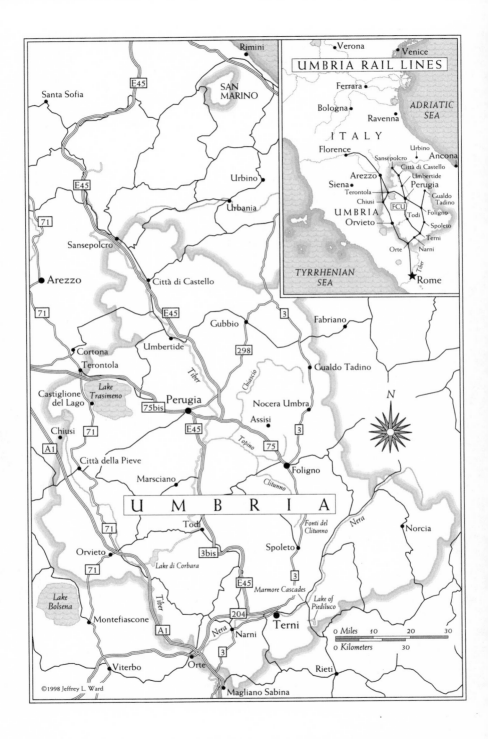

Umbria

Italy's

Timeless Heart

PAUL HOFMANN

Henry Holt and Company • New York

Henry Holt and Company, Inc.
Publishers since 1866
115 West 18th Street
New York, New York 10011

Henry Holt® is a registered trademark of
Henry Holt and Company, Inc.

Library of Congress Cataloging-in-Publication Data

Hofmann, Paul, 1912–
Umbria: Italy's timeless heart / Paul Hofmann.
p. cm.
ISBN 0-8050-4678-X (hardcover: alk. paper)
1. Umbria (Italy)—Description and travel. I. Title.
DG975.U5H66 1999
945'.65—dc21   98-34722

Henry Holt books are available for special promotions and
premiums. For details contact: Director, Special Markets.

First Edition 1999

Designed by Kelly Soong Too

Printed in the United States of America
All first editions are printed on acid-free paper. ∞

1 3 5 7 9 10 8 6 4 2

Contents

Contents

Italy at Its Best

Almost daily between Easter and late October, and every week during the rest of the year, travel organizations in Florence and Rome take busloads of visitors on much-advertised tours of the Umbrian hill towns. There would be plenty of those to choose from; most of the ninety cities and towns of the verdant region in the core of Italy sit on Apennine peaks or ridges, or climb from a valley onto slopes.

Yet the participants in those bus trips are shown just a few of them, and always the same ones—Assisi, Perugia, and Orvieto, perhaps Spoleto and Todi as well—and they only glimpse some others from the highway. The tourists are steered to souvenir emporiums bulging with majolica, other painted earthenware, and lace scarves, and they may lunch on reheated pizza, although Umbria is renowned for genuine, wholesome food.

The excursionists will bring back snapshots of some massive archway that they were told the Etruscans (Who were *they*?) erected 2,500 years ago, of ruined Roman arenas and medieval castles, of frescoed Gothic cathedrals and Renaissance palaces. They will have evanescent memories of vineyards, terraced olive groves, and the flaming yellow of sunflower fields in valleys bordered by hillsides with oak and pine forests. The tourists may or may not realize that they saw Italy at its best and most authentic.

Travelers of a different stripe have for centuries flocked to the Umbrian shrines dedicated to medieval religious figures. Generations before Chaucer told of his pilgrims merrily journeying to Canterbury, pious devotees of St. Francis and St. Clare already trekked to Assisi. The remote town of Norcia had won fame even earlier as the birthplace of St. Benedict, who championed the "pray and work" movement of monks that is credited with salvaging rudiments of civilization during the Dark Ages in Europe.

In the mountains south of Norcia, at Cascia, supplicants from all over Italy and even from abroad implore St. Rita, the "saint of the impossible," for help in desperate cases. And romantic couples from as far as America and Japan travel to the sanctuary outside the city of Terni where St. Valentine, the heavenly protector of lovers, is buried. Churches all over the region jealously guard their own relics. Umbria has since ancient times had a reputation for mysticism—but also, as will be seen, for black magic.

Then there is the foreigners' Umbria. Spoleto, on a slope that was inhabited already by prehistoric tribes, becomes a cosmopolitan rendezvous every June and July during the Festival of Two Worlds, one of Europe's more prestigious music and dance galas. What's more, many expatriates from the United States, Britain, and other countries have lately settled in or near Todi and other towns of the region, and consider them their new homes.

The real estate promoters who in their advertisements in newspapers abroad offer long-deserted, dilapidated farmhouses for sale tell the truth for once when they tout Umbria as the "gentle sister of Tuscany." In comparison with the region centering on proud Florence, overrun by foreigners, Umbria indeed appears unassertive, even humble, a poor relation. While many Tuscans are articulate, strong-willed, given to self-glorification, and are at times inclined to indulge in snobbery, Umbrians tend toward understatement and often seem withdrawn. It took an Italian-American with roots in the country's north rather than in Umbria, the composer Gian Carlo Menotti, to parlay Spoleto into a festival site of international importance.

⌣ Italy's Green Heart ⌣

Umbria, about two thirds the size of Connecticut, with barely 800,000 residents, is much smaller than Tuscany, its conspicuous neighbor to the northwest. The landscape of the two adjacent districts is similar: soft-contoured hills overgrown with cypresses, pines, oaks, diverse evergreens, and shrubbery; vineyards on the slopes and in the fertile, well-tilled valleys. Only a few higher mountains stand out. Umbria, with its many meadows, its livestock, and its more extensive woods, appears more rural than Tuscany. Because of its abundant vegetation and its peculiar shape on the map (a notched clump in the upper middle of the Apennine peninsula), Umbria has long been called the "green heart of Italy."

The Tiber traverses Umbria from north to south for 194 miles before reaching Latium and emptying into the Tyrrhenian Sea. Most of the time the river looks unimpressive, but when the rains come its level may suddenly rise by ten feet or more; it will spill over its banks, flood fields, and carry trees and drowned sheep downstream with it. Tributaries from the Apennines in the East pour much water into the Tiber. Umbria's rivers have since the oldest times driven flour and oil mills, and now generate more hydroelectric power than the region needs for itself.

Landlocked Umbria has a nearly continental climate with cold, often freezing, winters and hot summers. Westerly winds from the Tyrrhenian Sea usually bring rain in November and December. In the cold season snow often covers the summits and ridges, and every now and then also visits the hill towns, making their stairways and steep streets slippery, blanketing their roofscape, and coifing their many towers and domes.

Earth tremors are relatively frequent in Umbria, caused by shifting rock formations along fault lines evidenced in satellite photos. The districts of Gubbio, Spoleto, and, particularly, Norcia-Cascia suffered major earthquakes during the nineteenth and twentieth centuries.

An earthquake of medium intensity jolted Umbria and the neighboring region of the Marches in September 1997. It was followed by more than 8,000 aftershocks—some of them relatively strong, others only recorded by seismographs—over several months. A dozen persons were killed during the tremors, which were particularly severe in the districts of Foligno, Assisi, Gualdo Taldino, and Nocera Umbra. Many hundreds were made homeless and had to be temporarily housed in prefabs.

The damages to Umbria's artistic and architectural patrimony attracted worldwide attention to an emergency that, as earth-quakes go, wouldn't otherwise have hardly made headlines: The worst shocks were classified as being a 5.5 on the Richter scale or a IX on the Modified Mercalli scale.

The most illustrious victim of the Umbrian temblors of 1997–98 was the Basilica of St. Francis in Assisi, the repository of priceless thirteenth-century frescoes. Restoration work started immediately; the famous church was trussed into steel scaffolding that was to remain in place for a number of years.

During the quake scare, the farmers—even those whose homes had been destroyed—kept tilling their fields, vineyards, and olive groves and taking care of their domestic animals the way their forebears had done for thousands of years.

Wine and olives are grown all over Umbria as they are in Tuscany. These two cultures, quintessential for Mediterranean civilization, were probably first introduced in the Italian peninsula by Phoenician and Greek mariners and colonists around 800 B.C., maybe even earlier, and vastly expanded by the Etruscans later.

Wild animals roamed the Umbrian countryside and woodland until fairly recently. One of the best-loved legends about St. Francis of Assisi has the meek saint with uncharacteristic sternness order a man-eating wolf near the town of Gubbio to mend its savage ways. Various Umbrians who love the outdoors have told me that even now there are isolated wolves and wild boars in out-of-the-way spots in the region. Migratory birds choose Umbria as their winter quarters or as a stopover on their way to or from points farther south.

The many local hunters have lately met with increasing opposition from environmentalists. Bovines and sheep are bred throughout the region, pigs above all in its southeastern part around Norcia.

Umbria is one of the few areas in Italy where the population exodus from the countryside has been contained. There are no ghost towns like, for instance, those of the northern Apennines between Florence and Bologna. Quite a few urban families own land and, although they may have sold their ancient farmhouses to foreigners, will make sure that the fields remain cultivated by sharecroppers, that the grapes are harvested and the olives are picked and pressed.

The new settlers from abroad usually upgrade their properties, installing modern kitchens, bathrooms, heating systems, air-conditioning, and appliances at a cost that will be a multiple of the purchase price. Former city slickers may for a while, more or less successfully, dabble in farming if some land came with the deal. Apart from such uncertain experiments, Umbria still has a strong agricultural base. Most Umbrians vaunt rural roots, talk knowledgeably about farming and cattle-breeding problems, and will worry about what the vagaries of the weather mean for the economy of the countryside.

The cities have not grown excessively. The biggest of them, which is the regional capital, Perugia, has a population of 144,000. (Florence in comparison has more than 400,000.) The power plants, steel works, machine shops, and other factories in Terni, with a little more than 100,000 inhabitants, are Umbria's strongest industrial concentration. Also noteworthy are food-processing enterprises near Perugia, and small or medium-sized furniture, textile, and chemical ventures scattered around the region. Ceramics has been a cottage industry for centuries.

Umbria's solid agricultural foundation is reflected in its cuisine. Most of the cooking is done with its renowned olive oil. The wheat bread looks so crisp, smelling and tasting so good, that visitors are tempted to take a loaf with them.

Farro, or spelt (*Triticum spelta*), is a hardy variety of wheat that was cultivated in Umbria since the oldest times, and to this day is variously used in the region's frugal cuisine. The grain, which will thrive also on marginally fertile soils, was brought to Italy from the Near East, possibly by the Etruscans, and became a staple food of the early Romans. Spelt porridge was generally eaten by them before they knew bread. *Puls,* a kind of mush or polenta made of spelt, was used in sacrifices to the gods and as feed for the sacred geese and chickens. Today *minestra di farro,* meaning spelt soup, or a spelt porridge as a side order with pork, is offered by many Umbrian eating places, especially in Spoleto and Norcia— a link with prehistoric eating habits.

Pasta, ubiquitous in Umbria as it is in all other parts of Italy, often comes as thick noodles, known as *ombrici* in Perugia and Orvieto, or in broad strips. Narrower pasta bands are a Spoleto specialty, locally called *strangozzi* or *strozzapreti.* The latter term means "priest-strangler"; nobody could tell me whether the sardonic name meant that greedy churchmen could choke by stuffing themselves with that pasta variety, or that the shape of the noodles suggested the ropes by which one could get rid of unworthy members of the clergy. The "priest stranglers," at any rate, are often garnished with asparagus sauce in spring, or with peas, mushrooms, or, that Umbrian delicacy, truffles.

Gnocchi (small dumplings) are preferably made with the tasty local potatoes rather than with flour. Pasta dishes are frequently served with rich sauces that may be strengthened with eggs, soft cheese, mushrooms, or black or white truffles.

High-quality pork reaches the region's tables either roasted or as ham or in sausages. One popular treat is *porchetta,* an entire young pig, emptied of innards and seasoned with salt, pepper, garlic, wild fennel, and other herbs, then spit-roasted over a wood fire. The meat is eaten hot, and what remains may yield cold cuts for days. In addition to the Umbrian pork, also tender lamb, veal, and beef are available in most eating places. As for chicken, it is still possible to get the free-range variety, especially in villages and smaller towns. Many restaurant menus furthermore list pigeon, rabbit, and, during the hunting season beginning in September, venison.

The vast Lake Trasimeno and the region's streams furnish trout, mullet, eel, and other freshwater fish, but restaurants now get most of such provisions from hatcheries. I have seen vast fish farms on the upper Nera, a main tributary of the Tiber.

Almonds, figs, raisins, and candied fruits play a big role in the region's traditional desserts. Umbria's best figs are said to come from the small town of Amelia. The chocolate industry of Perugia, founded at the beginning of the twentieth century, exports its confections, including its well-promoted Perugina kisses (Baci), to the United States and other countries.

Among Umbria's wines, the whites from the Orvieto district are best known elsewhere in Italy and abroad. The areas around Lake Trasimeno, near Assisi, and, especially, around Montefalco too produce excellent vintages.

◡ː *Etruscan Heritage* ː◠

Flint arrowheads, hand axes, daggers, and other rock tools and weapons unearthed in various spots in Umbria and displayed in its museums prove that the region was inhabited at least since the younger Stone Age. We don't know anything about the original cave dwellers, and very little about the people that settled in the region between 2000 and 1000 B.C. The newcomers probably arrived from the North, crossing the Alps by various routes. The Greeks much later called them *Ombrikoi;* they spoke a language kindred to archaic Latin. An important, though late, recording of the Umbrian language is on seven bronze tablets treasured by the Civic Museum of Gubbio.

At one period the early Umbrians were spread over a wide area across central Italy, apparently from coast to coast. They were eventually pushed back by Adriatic tribes in the East and by the Etruscans in the West into what is the present landlocked region.

You hear a lot about the Etruscans in Umbria. The ever fascinating—because elusive—people made their appearance on the Italian west coast after 1000 B.C. and were known as Tyrrhenians to the Greeks; the Romans called them Tuscians or Etrurians, and eventually Etruscans. The Greek historian Herodotus, writing in the fifth century B.C., reported that the Tyrrhenians had migrated from Lydia in west-central Asia Minor to Smyrna (now Izmir), constructed ships, and "after sailing past many countries came to Umbria where they built cities for themselves."

Most scholars today tend to assume that the Etruscans indeed arrived in Italy from the Near East, very probably in small batches over considerable time. Some nineteenth-century historians instead held that the Etruscan immigration or invasion had taken place by land from the North. A modern Italian school of thought postulates that the puzzling people had its origin in the Apennine peninsula itself. The problem with this theory of indigenous roots is the Etruscan language—it is totally different from any of the idioms spoken at the time of its first appearance by the many tribes making up the Italian ethnic mosaic; Etruscan is also unrelated to such European splinter languages as Albanian or Basque. Instead, similarities with an ancient pre-Greek tongue that was spoken in the Aegean island of Lemnos have been detected.

Despite insistent scholarly efforts over several generations, the Etruscan language remains largely obscure. Aside from several thousand inscriptions (many of them found in Umbria), only very few Etruscan texts of any length exist. One of them is, curiously, on a papyrus shroud into which an Egyptian mummy was wrapped; the precious 1,200-word Etruscan document, dealing with religious ritual, is now in Zagreb, Croatia. The 7,000 or so known Etruscan words are mainly common names, most of them in funerary inscriptions, like "I am the tomb of Velelia." Nobody can tell which is which of the six numerals on Etruscan gambling dice.

If the Etruscans possessed any literature, it has been lost. Some of their murals show books that folded accordion-like and may have contained religious material; they must have crumbled into dust. The extreme scarcity of written evidence left by the unquestionably gifted Etruscan people, compared to the wealth of Greek and Latin literature that has come to us, has exasperated scholars for centuries.

Long before Rome entered on the stage of history, the Etruscans, early masters of metallurgy, supplied the peoples around the Mediterranean, and occasionally also those north of the Alps, with copper and iron helmets, armor, and swords. They turned out such equipment in their workshops on the Tuscan mainland facing the iron-rich island of Elba. The Etruscans traded their coveted military hardware for painted vases, sculptures, and other luxuries from Egypt and, especially, from Greece. They also acquired knowledge and know-how—including the Greek alphabet—and transmitted what they had learned to the indigenous peoples of Italy.

Gibbon acknowledged over 200 years ago that "Italy was indebted for the first rudiments of civilized life" to the Etruscans. Today it is generally acknowledged that they gave rise to the first high civilization in the peninsula. Apparently they were only a thin aristocratic upper class ruling over multitudes of farmers, shepherds, fishermen, artisans, and slaves. The Etruscans taught them how to efficiently tend the vines and olive trees, to build archways and aqueducts, to dig wells and sewers, to forge metal implements, to rig ships, to throw dice, to make and play musical instruments, and to forecast the future from the flight of birds and the entrails of sacrificed animals.

Politically the Etruscans never merged into a centralized state. Theirs was a cluster of cities and towns that they had either founded or taken over from their original inhabitants, and the surrounding land. These territorial units were governed by independent chiefs who allied with one another on special occasions, like war with their perpetual rivals, the Greeks. At one time in the sixth century B.C., Rome was under Etruscan control while Etruscan influence reached to the Naples area in the South and to the Alpine foothills in the North. Etruscan mariners and pirates were dominant in a vast expanse of the Mediterranean.

In central Italy a confederation of twelve Etruscan cities seems to have had mainly religious importance. In what is today Umbria, the Etruscans were prevalent west of the Tiber, and strongly influenced the Umbrians east of the river where they also had a few colonies.

Etruscan power waned as fast as it had grown. An Etruscan fleet was routed by Greek admirals in 474 B.C.; Etruscan chiefs were ousted from Rome; and the rising Roman Republic started gobbling up Etruscan city-states, along with the surviving Umbrian centers, one after another. Soon the Etruscans disappeared from recorded history. Yet they surely live on in the genetic and cultural endowment of the Italians in the heart of the peninsula, much the way Etruscan walls, water conduits, and wells still form an impressive texture to the subsoil of such Umbrian cities as Orvieto and Perugia.

It is mainly through their art—tomb frescoes and sculptures—that the Etruscans speak to us today. Much of what is visible now was still underground when D. H. Lawrence wrote his *Etruscan Places* in 1930, but his insights remain valid. He was struck by the gaudy wall paintings in the Etruscan burial chambers that were then known. Those frescoes picture earthy, playful, serenely smiling men and women *together* at table (very un-Roman and un-Greek in the fifth and fourth centuries B.C.!); contented-looking slaves (maybe Umbrians) and benignant masters; affectionate couples; players of the double flute and sensuous dancers; wrestlers, jugglers, and charioteers—all patently having a good time 2,500 years ago.

Beside all this good living, the Etruscans were intensely death-conscious and fascinated by magic and by what they imagined as the netherworld; this is evidenced by their elaborate tombs, by their typical reliefs of the funeral cortege's touching farewell to the deceased, and by other imagery. "Mystical" Umbria may have Etruscan roots.

Lawrence detected "the current of some strong different life" sweeping through the Etruscans, "different from our shallow current today; as if they drew their vitality from different depths that we are denied." The English author made a case for the present-day Italians really being more Etruscan than Roman: "sensitive, diffident, craving really for symbols and mysteries, able to be delighted with true delight over small things, violent in spasms, and altogether without sternness or natural will-to-power." His characterization fits many Umbrians.

The Etruscan strain in the makeup of the Italian personality may resemble one of those karst rivers that seep away into limestone caves, flow on as underground streams, and reemerge at some distant point as if springing from a new, mighty source. It is surely no mere coincidence that the Italian Renaissance originated in once-Etruscan domains, Tuscany and Umbria.

Giotto, the Florentine, painted his great Franciscan frescoes in Assisi, and a Tuscan-Umbrian artist, Luca Signorelli, decorated the Cathedral of Orvieto with powerful murals. Signorelli and his teacher Piero della Francesca were born close to the present border between Tuscany and Umbria; Michelangelo's birthplace, the village of Caprese, is nearby. Raphael, a native of Urbino just a few miles east of Umbria, received his early training in Perugia and did work also in Città di Castello on the upper Tiber before moving on to Florence. Perugia claims him as the foremost representative of the Umbrian School of painting; its masters, in addition to his teacher Perugino, include also Pinturicchio, Benozzo Gozzoli, Lo Spagna, and many minor artists.

Sweetness of expression in the human—especially female—face, harmonious composition, and an air of serenity characterize Umbrian frescoes, altarpieces, and canvases. The region's smiling landscape and sometimes its towns (as in Raphael's celebrated Madonna of Foligno) provide evocative backgrounds.

Speculation as to how much of the Etruscans' skills in the arts, craftsmanship, husbandry, and, presumably, gastronomy were transmitted to the people who today inhabit their former territory is fascinating, though futile.

✌ Invaders and Feuds ✌

Rome's piecemeal conquest of the Etruscan and Umbrian cities started in the fifth century B.C. and was barely completed when the ambitious and rapacious republic on the lower Tiber was to face the mortal danger of big-power aggression. Carthage's brilliant general Hannibal marched from Spain, crossed the Alps with his troops and elephants, and invaded central Italy. He destroyed two Roman legions on Lake Trasimeno in 217 B.C.; some of the Umbrian towns recently conquered by Rome defected to the Punic military genius, others, like Spoleto, rebuffed him. Eventually the fortunes of the Punic wars would turn.

Under long Roman domination Umbria throve economically and experienced a construction and engineering boom. Many ruins of temples, amphitheaters, bridges, aqueducts, and once-opulent private villas all over the region are enduring proof of great prosperity under the Romans. One of the strategic roads that the consuls of the Roman Republic built, the Via Flaminia, cut across Umbria, linking Rome with the Adriatic Sea and the northern plains; in some sections it incorporated old Umbrian and Etruscan tracks and paths. Today National Route No. 3 still follows the ancient highway in long stretches and is generally called by the name of the Roman road's creator in 220 B.C., Gaius Flaminius. The modern Via Flaminia, lined by service stations and motels, remains one of Italy's main arteries and an Umbrian lifeline.

Before the nation's network of modern motorways, the *autostrade*, were built after World War II, the Via Flaminia was even more vital than it is today. As recently as 1950 many motorists traveling between Rome and the north of the country would prefer to take the Via Flaminia with its comparatively few and easy mountain passes rather than the Via Cassia (National Route No. 2) by way of Siena and Florence and the mountain roads and tricky passes between that city and Bologna.

The web of highways laid out and well maintained by the Romans facilitated the barbarian onslaughts that hastened the decline and fall of their empire. Umbria was a favorite invasion route of Germanic tribes. One of the Teutonic peoples that poured into Italy, the Longobards or Lombards, established a dukedom in the core of the region, centered on Spoleto on the Via Flaminia, in A.D. 571. The mighty duchy lasted for hundreds of years. If today you run into a blond Umbrian, standing out in a population that is predominantly dark-haired, you may presume Germanic bloodlines.

The Middle Ages were for Umbria an era when great Romanesque and Gothic churches were built, and frequent fights erupted with new invaders as well as between the region's cities themselves. In Perugia and other centers local factions were often at each other's throats in savage civil wars. While Tuscany under the Medici achieved independence, Umbria was eventually annexed into the States of the Church. The power of the Vatican over the region was, however, purely nominal at times; local despots and clans actually ran various cities and districts, and engaged in their own private wars. Even small towns often undertook military operations, joining alliances or attacking some neighbor on their own.

Talking to Umbrians in the places where they are at home, I was often struck by their grasp of local history. They speak about the Etruscans, Romans, Lombards, and their other ancestors in the Middle Ages and the Renaissance as if those remote forebears had lived only a couple of generations earlier, as if there surely must be some oldster still around who remembers having seen them as a child.

The old factionalism has survived to this day, if only as an element of folklore or as semihumorous bad-mouthing. Police are regularly called out when teams from two Umbrian towns face each other in a soccer stadium. In Assisi, the inhabitants of the uptown district are notoriously critical of the downtown people, but they make a peace of sorts with them in a May festival. Friends in Perugia and other Umbrian places seemed only half-joking when they assured me that the Terni people were really uncouth. In Spoleto you will hear that Foligno is boring and lacks refinement. And all other Umbrians seem to agree that "the Gubbians are crazy."

If a car with a TR (Terni) license plate is parked in Foligno or Perugia, or a PG (Perugia) car is in Terni, the owner on picking it up may find that it has been scratched or stripped of its hubcaps. Such vandalism doesn't ordinarily happen in Umbria to vehicles with other Italian or with foreign license plates. Since the early 1990s Italy has been gradually eliminating the indication of the province of registration from auto license plates—ostensibly to simplify computerized car tracking, but actually to remove a cause for tribal animosities such as the inter-Umbrian tensions, a remote and rather comical echo of deadly serious feuds in the Middle Ages and the Renaissance. However, by the end of 1998 the two-letter codes of the provinces were again officially back on automobile license plates. The police had found that witnesses of car accidents could remember license numbers better if they included the indication of a province.

After the Renaissance the papacy managed to tighten its control of Umbria. The long government of—often unpopular—churchmen is one of the sources of diffuse anticlericalism in the region. It is one of the ironies of present-day Italy that while Roman Catholic traditions, sanctuaries, and monasteries abound in "mystical" Umbria, the church and its priesthood don't have much influence there.

Umbria remained a province of the pontifical state until 1860, when it was occupied by Piedmontese troops and became a part of unified Italy. King Victor Emmanuel II of Sardinia-Piedmont, the first sovereign of the new Italian state, as well as Giuseppe Garibaldi, the hero of the Risorgimento (the movement for national liberation and unity), and Camille Benso Count Cavour, the political architect of Italian unification, are honored in Umbrian cities and towns with statues, plaques, and the names of streets, squares, and edifices.

In October 1922 Umbria was the scene of an event, the so-called March on Rome, that signaled the takeover of Italy by fascism. Mussolini, the leader (*duce*) of the Fascist Party, prudently stayed in Milan, his political base, while his top aides established an operational headquarters in Perugia. The fascist leadership gathered thousands of black-shirted members of the movement in the Umbrian capital and took them to Rome in trucks, buses, and cars. On their way across Umbria and Latium the black-shirt brigades were joined by thousands of sympathizers.

Mussolini was meanwhile asked by King Victor Emmanuel III by telegram to form a new government, and he traveled from

Milan to Rome in a railroad sleeper. The black-shirts' progress from Umbria to the national capital turned into a triumphal parade. Fascist rhetoric would later depict the 1922 March on Rome as a revolutionary action; in truth it was rather a mass junket. With it started more than two decades of dictatorship. Mussolini's regime would ever after give special consideration to *antemarcia* ("before the March") fascists, meaning those—including many Umbrians—who had been party members before October 1922. Millions joined fascist organizations later.

Following Mussolini's downfall in 1943, Italian resistance fighters in the hills of Umbria, as elsewhere in the center and north of Italy, attacked small detachments and the supply lines of the occupying German army. Nazi retaliation and atrocities were the consequence. The guerrilla actions, often magnified in hindsight, and the reprisal victims are recalled in many memorials paying tribute to the local *partigiani* (partisans).

After World War II Umbria was among the bulwarks of the Italian Communist Party. Several cities and towns in the region established formal cultural pairings with urban centers in the Soviet sphere, promoting reciprocal group visits and other exchanges. The traveler arriving in Perugia, for instance, is informed by a road sign that the city is twinned with Bratislava, the Slovak capital.

Nobody was astonished nevertheless whenever the Communist mayor of some Umbrian town lent official municipal support to the traditional celebrations in honor of the local saint, and walked with the clergy and the faithful in the church procession climaxing the holiday. The collapse of the Soviet system has not much impaired left-wing strength in Umbria.

⌣ *Restrained Friends* ⌣

Even at the height of the Cold War, when the Italian Communist propaganda machine blasted the United States day after day, individual American tourists and the occasional American expatriate resident were always made to feel welcome in Umbria. Today, foreigners visiting the region or wanting to live in it will find quiet politeness and hospitality. Yet anyone who intends to settle will have to work at developing a close rapport or even friendship with local people.

The widely observable fact is that many Umbrians in dealings with outsiders—non-Italians and Italians alike—are reserved and often taciturn. Ask a dozen of their countrymen from other parts of the nation how they would characterize Umbrians in one word, and the term you will hear most often is *chiusi* (closed). Umbrians belie the stereotype of the outgoing, voluble Italian—the woman in the railroad compartment whom you have never met before, and who after half an hour tells you about her troubles with her mother-in-law, or the genial fellows in the trattoria who strike up a table-to-table conversation with a stranger and soon invite him to join and have a glass of wine with them.

Many people in the landlocked region seem at first standoffish or even defensive—like their ancient settlements, built on steep hills and ringed with stout walls. Whatever such apparent restraint may betray, timidity or diffidence, it will eventually melt if one proves to deserve trust. I am happy to report that over the years I have made a number of Umbrian friends—friends more dependable than many others in a country where the word is often used lightly, and whose language has a rhymed idiomatical adage, saying in translation, "God protect me from my friends—while from my enemies I'll protect myself."

As an off-and-on resident of Rome for half a century, I have made uncounted trips into Umbria to places just an hour or two distant from the capital. I have stayed for extended periods in various parts of the region. In preparation of this book I revisited most of Umbria's cities and towns. A knowledgeable native of Spoleto, Romina Venturi (who lives now in Perugia), assisted me with research. Among the reference books consulted, the three-volume *L'Umbria Si Racconta—Dizionario* by Mario Tabarrini (Foligno, 1982) was most useful.

It is long ago that I made my very first trip into Umbria, visiting the region's city most easily accessible from Rome—Orvieto. My young wife and I decided we needed a break, and with our son, Ernesto, then just six months old, traveled from Rome northward by train. In Orvieto we put up in a small hotel on the outskirts where in that off-season period we were the only guests. The owner's family and the chambermaid fussed a lot about our baby. One day I rented a car for an outing, telling the driver who came with it to swing by the Cathedral before proceeding to the countryside. I wanted to see again the frescoes that I had admired on arrival, and we asked the driver to guard the sleeping baby in the car for a few minutes while my wife and I were in the church. We may have become more absorbed in the Luca Signorelli murals than just a few minutes; when we left the Cathedral we found a small crowd around the rented car, no driver, and Ernesto crying his head off behind locked doors.

We heard muttered invectives—*"genitori assassini"* (murderous parents) was one I remember to this day. I tried to explain that we had entrusted the baby to the driver, and that he had evidently locked the car before wandering off. We were believed only when the hapless character, who had gone for a drink, showed up a few minutes later. Now *he* was roundly scolded by the irate bystanders, and I had to defend him, pointing out that the infant had seemed sound asleep. Little Ernesto, soothed by his mother, promptly dozed off again, and we could start our tour of the vineyards and side valleys in the westernmost tip of Umbria.

Umbria

1

⌣∴⌣

The Splendors of Orvieto

As half a dozen explosives experts of the Italian Army were gingerly working for eight hours one day in 1995 to dispose of a five-hundred-pound TNT bomb that the British Royal Air Force had dropped on the railroad station of Orvieto during World War II, television and radio newscasts said, "The nation is cut in two." What actually was cut were the tracks of the two Florence-Rome rail lines, the Motorway of the Sun, and the highways flanking and joining it—the principal surface connections between Northern Italy and the capital and the south of the country.

The bomb, more than half a century old, had been discovered when a railroad worker operating a bulldozer to prepare the ground for an additional marshaling-yard siding hit it, miraculously without being blown up. The bomb squad, called to the spot at once, ordered the railroad tracks and the roads within a large radius to be closed; three thousand people living in the neighborhood were temporarily evacuated.

After the grainy, gray TNT had at last been safely removed and the half-inch-thick steel container was nothing but a chunk of scrap metal, the Prefect of Terni Province, Giuseppe Civiate, whose jurisdiction includes Orvieto, joked: "We'll send the empty shell to the Queen of England with a bill for our trouble." The trains started running again, and traffic on the Motorway of the Sun, Italy's main north-south lifeline, resumed with a roar.

The bomb that since 1943 or 1944 had been slumbering under two feet of gravel and earth before being dismantled while people at a safe distance held their breath caused hardly a ripple in Orvieto proper. Nobody was evacuated in the ancient city of 21,000 inhabitants 650 feet above the rail station in the plain; Orvieto, enthroned on its rock of tufa that a Pleistocene volcano had spewed out, remained aloof as it did so often during its long history.

From their car or the windows of their train, millions of travelers every year catch a glimpse of the steep, elongated hump on which Orvieto rests, of its gray-brown skyline from which a few squat towers stick out, and of the tall facade of its wondrous cathedral. They fleetingly behold one of the most remarkable cities in a country full of urban marvels. Located not quite halfway between Florence and the Italian capital, Orvieto is the city of Umbria that is, at least by sight, best known to Italians and foreigners alike, although many ignore that it belongs to that region, whose westernmost outpost it is.

Sightseers who do go up to the lofty city usually just visit the cathedral, stroll a while in the narrow streets and lanes of the medieval quarter, perhaps have a meal or snack, and leave again after a few hours. There is only a small hotel of some pretension in town, the Maitani off Cathedral Square; a few other inns and pensions are plain. At night Orvieto impresses by its quiet.

Many Orvietans commute to Rome, where they are enrolled in schools or have jobs, and quite a few eventually decide to move to the capital for good, to return to their native city only on weekends or even less frequently. A young woman in Spoleto who occasionally visits friends in Orvieto had this to say: "On some nights during the week Orvieto feels outright sad; if it weren't for the soldiers who are let out of their barracks in the evening the city would look deserted. We other Umbrians regard the Orvietans a little as traitors: They always rub in how close they are to Rome, how often they go to the capital and how familiar they are with it."

Others instead cherish the signally unhectic pace of Orvieto and seek to explore the secret life of this urban island on the forbidding cliffs that often in history made it look unconquerable. It is a place for someone who wants to paint in its stupendous light, or write or study or just meditate.

The best and fastest trains of the Italian State Railways don't stop in Orvieto. The tracks of the Florence-Rome *direttissima* high-speed line in fact run a few hundred yards northwest of the city's station, bypassing it as if with disdain. To travel by train to Ostia one has to take one of the—usually uncrowded—interregional (IR) trains departing from Florence and Rome every two hours and reaching the city's station, after several intermediate stops, in about an hour and a half. By car on the A-1 Motor Road (Autostrada del Sole, or Motorway of the Sun) the trip from either of the two big cities to Orvieto will take an hour or so.

It's a good idea to leave one's vehicle near the railroad station, because driving in the warren of twelve-feet-wide one-way streets in Old Orvieto on the hill can be a maddening experience, and parking space up there is very scarce.

For several years municipal buses used to provide a connection between the rail station and the city center over the two and a half rising miles of National Route No. 71 that snake up the hill. Now the old cable-car service has been reactivated with roomy gondolas and other new equipment. It whips passengers from the station square up to the northeastern tip of Orvieto in a few minutes; the ticket, which at my most recent visit cost the equivalent of 90 cents, also entitles the holder to riding the bus from the upper cableway terminal to the city center (Piazza della Repubblica) and to the cathedral.

✌ *Ancient Aerie* ∾

The brown, isolated tufa ridge above the broad valley of the Paglia River, a tributary of the Tiber, attracted security-minded settlers already in the Bronze Age, maybe even earlier. Bronze knives unearthed on the hill prove that what is today Orvieto was inhabited at least 1,000 years before Etruscans installed themselves on it. Those sixth- or fifth-century-B.C. newcomers to the primitive hilltop village founded a city, surrounded it with walls, dug wells, and built a network of aqueducts and sewers in the soft subsoil. Many remains of Etruscan engineering have been found as deep as thirty feet below the present surface.

Such are the frustrations of Etruscology that we don't know even the name of the original city. It may have been Volsinii, according to historical sources a thriving center and a member of the Etruscan confederacy that the Romans destroyed in 280 B.C. or 265 B.C. (the chronology isn't clear on this point). As in other episodes of their bit-by-bit conquest of Etruria, the Roman legionnaires brutally looted the subdued city before putting it to the torch, and are said to have carried off 2,000 statues; of all that plunder only one piece, a stone head in a Florentine museum, still exists. The surviving inhabitants of the doomed place moved to Lake Bolsena, twelve miles to the southwest, and founded a "New Volsinii." The site of the first Volsinii, made desolate by the Romans, became known as *urbs vetus* (old city), so the theory assumes, and over the centuries the Latin term was transformed into Orvieto. Some scholars believe that Orvieto was nothing less than the religious center of the Etruscan League.

An Etruscan necropolis, or large cemetery, stretches out on a slope some two hundred yards off the highway, linking the city with its rail station. It can be reached from the northeastern section of Orvieto on foot in about fifteen minutes or by municipal bus if at least ten passengers ask the driver to extend the run to the sign NECROPOLI ETRUSCA on the highway.

The empty tomb chambers, hewn into the soft stone in various rows, are from the fifth century B.C. Several of the entrances to them, formed by slate gray tufa blocks under a foot-high blanket of earth and grass, carry the names of the dead in Etruscan characters. Greek vases and other artifacts found in the tombs were taken to museums in Orvieto, Rome, and elsewhere. Frescoed Etruscan tombs were discovered in the hillside about a mile south of Orvieto; their murals and other contents are now in Florence.

Ruins of an Etruscan temple near St. Patrick's Well (p. 20) and the upper terminal of the cable cars were dug up in the 1920s.

Looking at the gaping tomb chambers and at the mute exhibits in the collections, I always wondered, why did people of such evident high civilization leave no, or almost no, written legacy? Why did they have so little to say to posterity? No sacred books, no epics, no poetry, no chronicles, no treatises on agriculture or architecture, about which they knew so much, no law codes—just those directives on religious ritual and the brief funeral inscriptions. We possess more revealing data about some much older Middle Eastern civilizations from their cuneiform tablets than about how Etruscan society worked.

The lack of any literature, of course, favors the proliferation of theories concerning the origin, cultural achievements, history, and destiny of the people who for centuries lived—quite well at times, it appears—in Tuscany, Umbria, Latium, and beyond. "Mysterious" is the buzzword that seems inescapable whenever the Etruscans are mentioned. To me, a major mystery was always that they disappeared so quickly and seemingly so completely. Or did they?

In Orvieto, for instance, one notices many dark-haired people who, if they were wearing a purple-hemmed toga, might well figure in an Etruscan fresco. One of that kind was Luigi Barzini Jr., the author of the successful book *The Italians* (1964); he descended from an Orvieto family, and until mature age matched the romance writer's cliché description of "darkly handsome." When I once told him, "You are an Etruscan," he appeared pleased and replied, "Many people say so."

The Roman soldiery must have done a thorough scorched-earth job when they devastated the Orvieto of the Etruscans. For several centuries the place was never mentioned in any of the chronicles that have come to us, although the tempting hill cannot have remained totally abandoned for long. Former inhabitants or their descendants probably drifted back, and during the barbarian invasions people living in the nearby plains sought a refuge on the tufa hump. In the sixth century A.D. the troops of the Byzantine general Belisarius and the Ostrogoths fought over possession of what had again become a stronghold. Later other Teutonic warriors, the bearded Lombards who had already taken possession of Spoleto, also installed themselves in Orvieto.

The papacy eventually took control of the city. Locally, Orvieto was torn by feuds between aristocratic clans, as mentioned in Dante's *Divine Comedy*. Various pontiffs during the Middle Ages and the Renaissance sought safety in Orvieto when they felt threatened in Rome. A somber, battlemented edifice of dark tufa on the right (south) side of the cathedral, built in the thirteenth century, is known as the Palace of the Popes. Today it houses the Diocesan Museum, containing many items connected with the Cathedral.

That palace adjoining Orvieto's cathedral served as a temporary shelter for the Borgia pope, Alexander VI, in 1495 in a diplomatic-military hide-and-seek game with King Charles VIII of France. The young French sovereign, leading a formidable army into Italy, had humiliated Florence and the pope in Rome and had conquered Naples. Overextended supply lines, sagging troop morale, and venereal disease (the "Neapolitan malady") forced Charles, after a delicious spring in Naples, to return to France. The king wanted another meeting with the pope to nail down his conquests diplomatically, but Alexander VI who, apart from his notorious immorality was a shrewd politician, withdrew to Orvieto with twenty cardinals in order to evade such an encounter. When the French king arrived there with his forces to catch up with the pontiff, he found to his pique that the Spanish pope had moved to Perugia. Charles gave up and proceeded on his long march home, during which he still managed to inflict a disastrous defeat on the army of an Italian coalition in a brief, bloody battle at Fornovo in the northern Apennines.

Another pope, Clement VII, repaired to Orvieto in a much more desperate condition thirty-two years later, disguised as a peddler. Clement, a member of the Florentine House of Medici, had been a virtual prisoner in his fortress overlooking the Tiber near the Vatican, the Castel Sant'Angelo, for six months after the horrendous Sack of Rome by the German-Spanish troops of Emperor Charles V, in 1527. The soldiers, many of whom were Protestants, had killed at least 10,000 Romans, committed innumerable other atrocities, and assiduously looted the city. The pope was allowed to flee only after paying a ransom of 150,000 ducats. As soon as the pontiff had recovered from shock and exhaustion, he ordered the construction of the deep water shaft that is now known as the Well of St. Patrick for fear that the imperial invaders would besiege Orvieto the way they had besieged his stronghold in Rome. They didn't, however, and the well remained the city's white elephant (p. 20).

↲ Corpus Christi City ↳

An earlier pope, Urban IV, gave orders in 1264 to erect a magnificent cathedral in Orvieto, and illustrious architects from Tuscany and Umbria worked on the project for hundreds of years. Urban IV, a Frenchman whose father had been a shoemaker, resided in the city during most of his pontificate, 1261–64. A miracle that had been reported from the nearby lake town of Bolsena in 1263 was the motivation for the giant building enterprise.

A priest from Bohemia, Peter of Prague, so the story goes, was plagued by doubts as to the doctrine of transubstantiation—the dogma that during mass bread and wine are transformed into the body and blood of Christ without changing their outward appearance. During a pilgrimage to Rome the skeptical cleric was convinced of the truth of this basic tenet of Roman Catholic faith: While saying mass on his way to Rome in the eleventh-century Church of St. Christine at Bolsena (which still exists), he noticed drops of blood oozing from the host he had just consecrated; the liquid also tainted the white linen cloth (the corporal) he was using in the celebration of the Eucharist.

Raphael pictured the scene in a famous fresco in the Stanze of the Vatican, 1512–14. When Pope Urban IV was informed by the Bohemian priest of the supposed miracle, he asked the bishop of Bolsena to verify it. Having received confirmation, the pontiff by his bull *Transiturus* instituted the feast of Corpus Christi, to be celebrated on the second Thursday after Pentecost (Whitsunday). The blood-stained corporal, or chalice cloth, of Bolsena is treasured in a reliquary in Orvieto Cathedral. It is exhibited to the faithful and carried through the streets of the city in a solemn procession at Corpus Christi (in Italy known as the feast of Corpus Domini).

At Pentecost, the seventh Sunday after Easter, a curious ceremony, the Festa della Palombella (Feast of the Little Dove), is enacted in front of the cathedral. A live white pigeon in a metal cage is lowered on a cable, spanned for the occasion between the roof of the Church of St. Francis, a few hundred yards to the west, and the steps leading up to the three portals of the cathedral. A salvo of hundreds of firecrackers is set off as the pigeon is making its short trip. The performance (now criticized by animal rights advocates), which goes back to the Middle Ages, was held inside the cathedral until last century; it symbolizes the descent of the Holy Spirit on the disciples of Jesus in Jerusalem (Acts, II).

Whitsunday and Corpus Christi, the peak of the Orvieto tourist season, are usually observed in the city also with secular pageants giving local people a chance for dressing up in medieval costumes, flaunting the coats of arms of leading families, and carrying the banners of the medieval craft guilds.

Sightseers arriving in Orvieto will usually head first of all for Cathedral Square (Piazza del Duomo) on the city's south side. It is a noble space around one of Italy's, indeed the world's, most celebrated Gothic churches. Like the cathedrals of Pisa, Siena, and Florence, the 343-foot-long edifice was built in alternating layers of dark and bright material—here volcanic basalt and yellow-gray, porous limestone, both quarried in the city's surroundings.

The austere, zebrine walls are offset by a 166-foot-high facade surmounted by three gables and enhanced by a magnificent rose window with elegant tracery, many sculptures, and mosaics. The lowest tier of the marble bas-reliefs, which the groping hands of visitors could reach, is protected by Plexiglas. The sculptural ornamentation of the facade was completed only in the seventeenth century, and work on the multicolored mosaics on gold ground went on for another 200 years.

For a good, long look, many visitors sit down on the door steps of the stately houses opposite the facade or on chairs put there for them, left and right of the narrow Via Maitani. It is named after Lorenzo Maitani of Siena (circa 1275–1330), one of the chief architects of the cathedral, who died in Orvieto. In the evenings on Sundays and feast days the facade is floodlighted, and seems to take on a life of its own, like a huge, luminous triptych in a museum, independent of the dark church behind it.

The bas-reliefs on the lower sections of the facade's four mighty pillars represent episodes from the Old and New Testaments. Above them are the emblems of the Four Evangelists in bronze—the lion of St. Mark, an eagle for St. John, an angel for St. Matthew, and an ox for St. Luke—executed by Maitani. That versatile artist, who was a painter and sculptor, too, besides excelling as an architect, also created the marble Madonna, flanked by bronze angels under a bronze canopy, above the Cathedral's middle portal.

The rose window by Andrea Orcagna of Florence (1359) has at its center a sculptured head of Jesus and is placed in a square formed by mosaics representing four Fathers of the Church and fifty-two heads of saints; there are also relief statues of twelve Old Testament prophets and the twelve Apostles. Exhaustive knowledge of the Scriptures and of church history is needed to decode such figurative wealth.

The mosaics above the three doors and in the three gables, with their vivid blues and bright gold grounds, look new; some are indeed modern, and the others have been repeatedly restored. The topmost gable composition, Coronation of the Virgin Mary, was executed between 1842 and 1847. The lower panels represent the Annunciation, the Presentation in the Temple, and the Baptism of Jesus. The bronze doors are by the Sicilian sculptor Emilio Greco, executed between 1961 and 1965. (An Emilio Greco Museum on Cathedral Square contains other works by the artist, and diverse paintings and sculptures by contemporaries.)

After the gorgeous sight of the facade with its exuberant stone ornaments, its marble figures and bronzes, and its gaudily colored mosaics with gold as the dominant, the interior of the cathedral will strike you as severe. From a pavement of reddish-brown stone slabs the pillars rise to the timber rafters like giant tree trunks with dark and light bark—the basalt and sandstone bands.

Repeated visits during several years in the 1980s and early 1990s disappointed me because the celebrated frescoes by Luca Signorelli, among the supreme achievements of Renaissance art, were each time inaccessible. A sign on a grate closing the Cappella Nuova (New Chapel) in the right transept stated that restoration work had been carried out, off and on, since 1848, and that in a general overhaul new equipment was being installed to control the microclimate inside the chapel, which is adorned with the precious murals.

For the equivalent of 60 cents a machine explained, in one of four languages to be selected, what might have been seen had the chapel been open. There were two earphones so that a couple could listen simultaneously. Color slides were flashed on a little screen, but the trouble was that the taped comments, lasting three minutes, were running ahead of the pictures. Visitors who hadn't had the good fortune—as I had enjoyed many years earlier—of seeing the frescoes in the original could look at picture post-cards or at reproductions available in the souvenir shops near the cathedral.

Then, in the spring of 1996, by a stroke of luck, I was able to view the Signorelli frescoes from a much closer distance than most sightseers ever will. As the latest restoration drive was nearing completion and the scaffolding in the chapel was about to be dismantled, the art officials in charge of the project had decided to permit small groups of visitors to climb up on it and see in detail what had been done. Thus, one morning I found myself with nine other sightseers on a wooden platform supported by a castle of steel tubes sixty feet above the floor of the chapel.

Giuseppina (Giusi) Testa, an expert from the central government's Superintendency of the Environmental, Architectural, Artistic, and Historical Patrimony of Umbria in Perugia, explained to us that the frescoes had long been damaged by the humidity of the ancient walls, by rashlike saline incrustations, and by red algae as well as by incompetent restoration attempts. The *dottoressa*, a slight, blond woman in blue jeans, said that the walls had at last been dried out and were now being continually monitored, while the algae had been eliminated chemically. Dr. Testa, who with a team of architects had for years been following the work in the chapel, deplored the ineffectual treatments in the distant past. At one time 150 years ago, it seems, artists on grants from the Academy of St. Petersburg in Czarist Russia had "cleaned" the chapel with brushes and soft bread, irremediably removing color in spots of the frescoes that Signorelli had painted.

Signorelli, whose real name was Luca d'Egidio di Ventura, was born in the hill town of Cortona, only a few miles north of Lake Trasimeno in Umbria, sometime between 1441 and 1450, and learned his art as a pupil of the great Piero della Francesca and of Perugino, together with the young Raphael. His dramatic conception of his pictorial themes marks a departure from the tenderness of the Umbrian School. As about the first Renaissance master who had no misgivings about painting female nudes not representing the biblical Eve, Signorelli may be considered a forerunner of Michelangelo, whom he influenced.

In 1499, after long negotiations with the Orvieto Cathedral

chapter, he undertook to complete the pictorial decorations of the "new" chapel for 180 ducats. The right transept is also known as the Chapel of the Madonna of St. Brizio (or St. Brixius), an Umbrian saint who may have been an early bishop of Spoleto and is the subject of many legends; he is supposed to be somehow connected with a miraculous painting of the Virgin Mary hanging in this part of the Orvieto Cathedral. Fra Angelico from Fiesole and his assistant Benozzo Gozzoli from Florence had started work in the chapel more than fifty years earlier, executing two panels showing Jesus and Prophets in a vaulting.

Signorelli, assisted by his son Polidoro and two other men, created his powerful Orvieto frescoes between 1499 and 1504. A cycle devoted to the general theme of the Last Judgment, they represent the Fall of the Antichrist, the Darkening of Sun and Moon, the Destruction of the World by Fire, the Resurrection of the Dead, the Punishment of the Damned, the Ascent to Heaven of the Blessed, and the Crowning of the Blessed. Signorelli painted his self-portrait at the side of Fra Angelico in a corner of the painting on the left wall where the overthrow of the Antichrist is pictured. Fra Angelico is shown in the austere black habit of the Dominican Order, to which he belonged, while Signorelli, who was known for his love of the good things in life, represented himself as wearing patrician clothes.

The mass of figures populating the scenes on the walls and on the ceiling are grouped into "choirs"—the choir of the martyrs, of the virgins, of the prophets, of the church fathers, etc. Medallions contain subsidiary characters like Homer, Virgil, Horace, Dante, and others, and scenes from their works. In his masterful compositions, with their nudes and bold foreshortenings, Signorelli spoke an artistic idiom that was completely new at the time.

Michelangelo borrowed several ideas from them for his Last Judgment in the Vatican's Sistine Chapel.

The cathedral's left transept, known as the Chapel of the Corporal—also under restoration, off and on—could be visited when I was last in Orvieto. The blood-stained linen cloth, testimony of the Miracle of Bolsena, is preserved there in a gilt silver reliquary, normally kept in a marble tabernacle that is flanked by two Baroque statues of archangels. The reliquary, which may have been designed by Maitani, was executed by a Sienese jeweler in 1338; it is four and a half feet high and two feet wide, weighing 300 pounds, its shape recalling the c18athedral's gabled facade. Enamel work on either side of the precious receptacle represents the miraculous event at Bolsena and biblical scenes.

The Miracle of Bolsena and developments after that occurrence are narrated also in a dozen scenes by the Orvietan painter Ugolino di Prete Ilario who, with his assistants, frescoed the walls of this chapel during the second half of the fourteenth century. The cycle was thoroughly repainted 500 years later and now looks almost like a modern copy. One of the panels shows Pope Urban IV commanding St. Thomas Aquinas to write the prayers for the Mass of the Most Holy Sacrament; the great Dominican theologian and philosopher was teaching at the Studium, or ecclesiastical academy, of Orvieto when the miracle was reported from Bolsena. To see the frescoes better, put some Italian coins in a slot, and the Chapel of the Corporal will light up for a few minutes.

The choir was filled with scaffolding during my latest visit to the cathedral. Its frescoes by minor fourteenth- and fifteenth-century painters, with possibly an occasional intervention by Pinturicchio, were being restored, and a provisional main altar had been erected on a carpeted dais in the central nave.

The Papal Palace (p. 9) on the right side of the cathedral, with an outside stairway leading to a balcony, carries the large inscription MUSEO (museum). The exhibits in its large second-floor hall include a Mary Magdalene attributed to Signorelli (1504), sketches by Maitani preparatory to work connected with the cathedral project, sculptures by the same master, and Madonnas by the fourteenth-century Sienese painter Simone Martini.

The Civic Museum opposite the cathedral's facade is noteworthy for its Etruscan sarcophagi with bas-reliefs, as well as for frescoes detached from the walls of Etruscan tomb chambers and various artifacts found in them. The museum is named after Claudio Faina, a member of a wealthy Umbrian family of landowners, civic leaders, and collectors of antiquities and art who in the nineteenth century was abducted by bandits and assassinated while negotiations for buying his freedom were still going on. Kidnappings for extorting ransom had long plagued the States of the Church, to which Orvieto belonged for centuries, while such crimes were endemic—and partly still are—in Southern Italy, Sicily, and Sardinia.

Before exploring the city, walk a few hundred yards from the right of the cathedral, past the Papal Palace, to a parapet commanding a fine view of a side valley. A former abbey down there goes back to the eleventh century. The complex, nearly four miles south of Orvieto, was restored in various epochs and, after partial restructuring, is now a luxury hotel with a park, a swimming pool, and tennis courts. The twelfth-century abbey church of San Severo e Martirio, which has been spared commercial exploitation, is remarkable for its tall twelve-sided campanile with a flat, crenellated top overlooking grassland and olive groves in the valley.

The Middle Ages seem to live on not only in and around the cathedral and other churches and monasteries, but in every neighborhood of Orvieto. Many buildings on the narrow streets and on the few squares are very old, even though their ground floors today may house chic boutiques. At some spots it is hard to tell what is a tufa outcrop and what is medieval masonry. Outwardly, the ancient city looks compact, and gray or brown—but peer into the doorways, and you will often glimpse greenery and flowers inside. The Orvietans have a knack for cultivating semisecret gardens in only a few square feet of a courtyard or terrace.

From the left side of the cathedral's facade the Via del Duomo leads to the cramped city center, intersecting with the Corso Cavour. This is the main shopping street, undulating for more than half a mile across the city from east to west. A 134-foot-high square clock tower faces the Via del Duomo. It is known as the Torre del Moro (Moor's Tower) because of the relief of an Arab's head nearby whose meaning has slipped from the collective memory; it is a beloved landmark. Various businesses, including a restaurant, are named after that Moor.

To the west of the central tower is the rectangular Piazza della Repubblica with the arcaded City Hall, which was started in the thirteenth century and is still uncompleted; the Orvietans like it that way. On its left is the Church of Sant'Andrea, in which Romanesque and Gothic style elements blend; its twelve-sided campanile resembles the tower of the former Abbey of San Severo in the valley south of Orvieto (p. 18).

Walking from the Moor's Tower through a short, narrow street northward, one reaches the Piazza del Popolo with a freestanding, imposing building of honey-colored tufa blocks from the thirteenth century with an external flight of stairs. In times of war Orvieto's citizens' militia used to assemble in this Palace of the People before marching out to face the enemy.

Strolling around the city, the visitor will notice several other ancient churches and many stately buildings, often with much less impressive old houses huddling next to them. The so-called Medieval Quarter in the northeastern part of Orvieto, closest to the cable-car terminal, is a maze of crooked lanes and age-old dwellings.

✌ No Water from the Well ✌

The well that Pope Clement VII ordered to be built after the Sack of Rome in 1527 to enable Orvieto to withstand a possible siege never had to supply the city with water, but it nevertheless is an impressive achievement of Renaissance engineering. It was designed and started by the renowned Florentine architect Antonio da Sangallo the Younger, and completed by Simone Mosca, a sculptor and builder from the Florence region who did also much other work in Orvieto.

The shaft, in part hewn out of the perpendicular cliff and in part built in masonry, is 200 feet deep and sixteen and a half feet wide. It reaches the layer of clay soil beneath the tufa rock that carries Orvieto; the water at the bottom comes from an underground stream. Two parallel spiral staircases wind around the well; processions of mules were supposed to be driven down on one and return upward with their water-filled buckets on the other.

When the construction was finished after ten years of work, the danger of a siege had receded, and the city found it didn't need any water from the spectacular and costly well. The

Orvietans called the structure the Well of St. Patrick because it was declared to resemble the Holy Wells of Struell near Downpatrick, County Down, to which the sainted patron of Ireland is said to have withdrawn for prayer and penitence. Irish pilgrims must have come frequently through Orvieto on their way to or from Rome, and told local people the story of the revered caves in their faraway island. In Italian the term *Pozzo di San Patrizio* (Well of St. Patrick) has long become an idiomatic phrase denoting a thing or person that continually swallows or demands money without ever producing any worthwhile result, like a chronically money-losing business or a perpetual student who never graduates.

St. Patrick's Well can be visited, and I once descended all its 248 steps and climbed up again on the alternate stairs. The steps down are easy, but on returning to the surface I found that 248 of them are quite a lot. At the bottom of the well I shivered in the chill. The circular wall of the shaft is overgrown with moss; dim light penetrates through seventy-two windows. Many sightseers just remain at the well's mouth and look into the deep. The masonry part of the construction emerging from the tufa cliff is visible from the railroad and the highway in the valley.

Near the entrance to St. Patrick's Well on the northeastern tip of Orvieto and the upper terminal of the cable-car system is the Municipal Park on the site of a long-ruined fourteenth-century fortress, La Rocca (The Stronghold). It was built on orders from Gil Alvarez Cardinal Albornoz (circa 1300–1367), a formidable Spanish churchman who restored papal authority in Rome and central Italy, including Umbria, while the popes were residing in Avignon, southern France. The readers of this book will again encounter Cardinal Albornoz—the consummate administrator, diplomat, and strategist—in various other contexts; he dotted the region's hills with citadels.

A few hundred yards west of St. Patrick's Well are Italian Army barracks. Orvieto is the seat of one of the army's basic-training centers, and the battalions of recruits who are being initiated here into the rigors of military discipline every year provide business for local pizzerie and other trades. Old-timers, instead, fondly recall other, more glamorous youthful guests—the students of the Women's Academy of Physical Education that flourished in Orvieto from 1935 to 1944.

The institution was a pet project of Mussolini, who had a keen eye for female pulchritude. The 200 young women from all over the nation who, after painstaking selection, were admitted to the new school to be trained for jobs as gymnastics instructors or sports coaches fired the imagination of male Italians. In flattering blue-and-white uniforms especially designed for them, the Orvieto belles periodically pranced in Fascist Party parades in Rome and other cities, exciting much admiration, envy, and lust. They boarded and received their education in the disused, restructured Church of San Domenico, which was founded in the thirteenth century, and in adjacent buildings on the city's north side. "Orvieto was poorer when the girls had gone after the war," a white-haired souvenir vendor on Cathedral Square told me. "Now instead of them we have raw recruits with their first army haircuts."

The former Church of San Domenico belonged to a sprawling Dominican monastery that also included the area of the present army barracks. St. Thomas Aquinas lived and taught here during the years he spent in Orvieto while being formally attached to the papal court as its official theologian. The choir and some chapels of the Church of San Domenico have been preserved and can be visited. One chapel contains the pulpit from which St. Thomas Aquinas is said to have lectured. On the old altar is a crucifix of wood that, according to legend, once spoke to the saintly scholar. It seems that Thomas Aquinas heard himself addressed by the crucifix in Latin instead of the Aramaic or Hebrew that Jesus is supposed to have spoken: *"Bene scripsisti de me, Thomas!"* (You wrote well about me, Thomas!)

The army barracks in the former Dominican monastery generate much traffic of military personnel in and out of the city. Fledgling soldiers periodically crowd the Orvieto railroad station deep below. The railyard is surrounded by a cluster of service stations, road houses, unassuming hotels, and a few modern residential buildings. The undistinguished low neighborhood is officially called Orvieto Scalo (*scalo* meaning railroad stop), and it is a good thing that it is quite separate from the ancient city on its tufa shelf.

ᴠᴄ Vineland ᴄᴠ

Orvieto looks out on vineyards all around. Wine has been grown in the valleys and on the hillsides here since Etruscan times; the straw-colored, often slightly sparkling, Orvieto is the choice product of Umbrian viticulture. It is based on trebbiano grapes and is traditionally marketed in paunchy bottles, although big wineries, like Bigi, now fill it up also in slim standard bottles that save space on supermarket shelves. As is true also of other popular vintages, Orvieto drunk where it is grown tastes gratifyingly different from what one picks from the wine list of some faraway restaurant or pours out of a bottle that has traveled overseas.

The Orvieto wine country extends for miles north of the city, and a side trip across it is pleasant and rewarding. Don't take the Motorway of the Sun (A-1), but drive, slightly to its east, on National Route No. 71. It cuts across vineyards, rows of olive trees, and, eventually, oak forests. The highway leads past the once-fortified village of Ficulle, with a battlemented medieval tower and ceramics stores, to the town of Monteleone di Orvieto on a panoramic spur overlooking the broad Chiana Valley.

The Etruscans are credited with having first regulated the Chiani River, a subtributary of the Tiber that pours its water into the Paglia River near Orvieto. The valley was a thriving farming area in ancient Roman times but silted up during the Middle Ages and is mentioned as a fever-plagued swamp in Dante's *Inferno*. Drained anew during the eighteenth century, the wide valley, criss-crossed by canals, is again most fertile today, a delight to look at.

Monteleone di Orvieto was founded in the eleventh century by Orvieto as an outlying stronghold to defend the city's northern possessions. Remains of the medieval fortifications are still visible. A mural in the choir of the Collegiate Church, showing a Madonna and Child between the Apostles Peter and Paul, is attributed to Perugino, but may actually be the work of a disciple.

Five miles farther to the north on National Route No. 71 is the town of Città della Pieve, the birthplace of Perugino (1446–1524). We shall meet this master of the Umbrian School of painting, whose real name was Pietro di Cristoforo di Vanni, or Vannucci, again in the city with which he was to become identified, Perugia (p. 50).

The largest work by Perugino in his native town is a fresco representing the Adoration of the Magi, painted by him for the Church of Santa Maria dei Bianchi in 1504. Copies of two letters by the artist, on display in the room where the fresco can be seen, show that he reduced his fee for the work from 200 to 75 florins. Perugino, who was egregiously business-minded, made clear that he granted the discount "as a *paisano*" (compatriot), and wanted a 20-florin advance. Other paintings by the master are in the cathedral: in the choir a Madonna with St. Peter, St. Paul, and the town's patrons, St. Gervase and St. Protase; and a Baptism of Jesus in the first chapel on the left.

The word *pieve* in the town's name means a major church that isn't the see of a bishop. An Etruscan settlement at the dawn of history, Città della Pieve is today a very quiet place of fewer than seven thousand residents in an enviable hillside position at 1,670 feet altitude near the border between Umbria and Tuscany. Nearly a mile of medieval fortifications with many turrets enclose it partially, the view from some points embracing the green Chiana Valley. Very few trains stop today at the Città della Pieve station of the old Rome-Florence line. To reach the town by rail, travel to Chiusi-Terme di Chianciano, then take the public bus from there to Città della Pieve, five miles distant.

"The last time anything was going on here was a rock festival on May Day; lots of young people from Perugia, Orvieto, and Tuscany came," a teenager ruefully told me in late summer. "Apart from that, nothing ever happens in Città della Pieve."

2

❦

Perugia Detour

Journeying from Florence to Rome by car or railroad, the traveler will be tempted to take the shortest route, passing Orvieto or, at most, stopping over briefly in that singular city. An enticing alternative, however, is the detour by way of Perugia, Assisi, Foligno, and Spoleto: It adds sixty miles and a great many delights to the itinerary. Stendhal, for one, said he preferred the Umbrian detour to the briefer road.

Motorists coming from the north leave the Motorway of the Sun (A-1) at its Valdichiana exit, proceeding on Superhighway 75-bis (*bis,* Latin for "twice," is the Italian code for an alternate highway) to Perugia; those driving northward from Rome who want to see more of Umbria after Orvieto whetted their appetite may leave the Autostrada A-1 at its Chiusi-Terme di Chianciano exit, head for National Route No. 71, and drive northward until they reach 75-bis.

Rail travelers can board a few direct trains to Perugia daily from either Florence or Rome by way of Terontola-Cortona; the interregional trains (IRs) shuttling between Florence and Rome every two hours stop in Terontola-Cortona where passengers will catch connecting trains to Perugia, Assisi, and Foligno.

Soon after turning east, the superhighway and train tracks coast the northern shore of Lake Trasimeno for more than ten miles. The lake, framed by a green garland of low hills, is fifty square miles large, twice the size of Manhattan. "It's our sea," many Umbrians will tell you—the landlocked region's vastest body of water for bathing and boating. Through the millennia until recently it was also a prime provider of eels, fat carps, and other freshwater fish; however, water pollution has lately deci-mated the aquatic fauna. I myself, while swimming in the lake off the town of Passignano, have seen dead fish floating belly-up in the water that had officially been declared safe for bathing. The Fishery Museum at the hamlet of Feliciano on the lake's eastern shore with its historic nets and tackle is a nostalgic reminder of a bygone lacustrine culture.

Migratory birds during their long passage from northern Europe to Africa in autumn and back again in spring still like to make a rest stop in the forests and olive groves surrounding Lake Trasimeno and on its three islands as well as in the reeds on its shores. The serenely beautiful scenery is in some stretches still the same that delighted Goethe and Byron. While such famous trav-elers praised the Umbrian lake, soberly minded Italians proposed to dry it up to gain new farmland. At one time Napoleon got interested in a proposal to drain the lake, but the French emperor's hold on Italy didn't last long enough for starting such an enterprise; in the second half of the nineteenth century the project was again taken into consideration by the government of newly unified Italy. Luckily, nothing came of it.

There is archeological evidence that Etruscan engineers 2,500 years ago already took measures to regulate the lake, which averages twenty feet deep, is fed by little streams and a few underground sources, and tends to flood after prolonged rains. The ancient Romans built a draining canal receiving water through an opening below the lake's present surface on its southeastern side. Since then, various canals were built, silted up, and were again repaired. At present an outlet from a southeastern bay channels water into the Tiber whenever flooding threatens.

Older inhabitants of the towns around the lake recall that in February 1960 it froze over and remained frozen for several days. Generally, however, the climate around Lake Trasimeno is soft.

On the western shore of the circular lake, sitting on a limestone promontory amid olive groves close to National Route No. 71, is the town of Castiglione del Lago, with medieval walls, a medieval castle with four towers, and a Renaissance ducal palace. In springtime every two years kiting enthusiasts hold an international rally there to fly their gaudily painted artificial birds in the updrifts from the lake. "Color the Sky!" is the motto of the periodic event.

✌ A Lake Trap ✌

Travelers who, at the town of Tuoro on the northern shore of Lake Trasimeno, leave the superhighway to take the old, and more picturesque, narrow road will see a modern bust of an African amid the trees—Hannibal (247–183 B.C.). The sculpture is a long-delayed tribute to a great enemy of Rome, and a memento of one of the worst defeats the Roman Republic suffered in one of history's famous military confrontations. More than 15,000 Romans, nearly the complete strength of two legions, died in the disaster.

The Battle of Lake Trasimeno in April of 217 B.C. is still being analyzed in military schools as a conspicuous example of the need for reliable intelligence and tactical reconnoitering, as well as of a successful commander's gift for seizing unforeseen opportunities.

Hannibal, who as a youth had sworn undying hatred of the Romans, started the Second Punic War from Carthage's colonies in Spain. After besieging and capturing Saguntum, an ally of the Roman Republic near what is now Valencia, Hannibal, in 218 B.C., marched across the South of France. As was the usage of the times, the Carthaginian general replenished his forces by recruiting men from the countries he traversed—Iberians, Gauls, and others. The core of his army were his loyal North Africans. In a spectacular logistical feat Hannibal crossed the Alps into Italy with an estimated 26,000 men, comprising foot soldiers and cavalry, and thirty-seven elephants.

The elephant detachment was led by two female pachyderms whom the other animals docilely followed. According to the Greek historian Polybius, their handlers were Indians, but the elephants themselves were almost certainly African. The altitudes of 6,000 feet or so at the Alpine passes with their rock slides and snow must have put a tremendous strain on the heavy tropical beasts; they arrived exhausted in the Northern Italian plains, and almost all of them died that winter.

In Northern Italy the Carthaginian general inflicted a smarting defeat on a Roman army and went into winter quarters somewhere near Bologna. In the spring of 217 B.C. Hannibal marched southward. He had lost the sight in one eye owing to an ailment, and was riding his only remaining elephant (whose name may have been Surus) across the swamps of the upper Arno Valley. His foot troops and cavalry had shrunk through diseases during the harsh months in the northern Apennines.

The Senate in Rome had sent two armies to stop the invaders. The Roman force closest to Hannibal was led by one of that year's two consuls, Gaius Flaminius, the builder of the highway from Rome to the Adriatic coast (Via Flaminia). The other army, under Consul Cnaeus Servilius, was futilely guarding the Adriatic shore road, far away. Flaminius was an outstanding statesman, but despite some military experience was no match for the Carthaginian leader.

Polybius (III, 83–84) relates how Hannibal, proceeding from the Etruscan-Roman city of Cortona, with feints set a trap for Flaminius on the northern shore of Lake Trasimeno, and how the Roman consul with his legions readily marched into it.

On a misty morning, such as are frequent on the lake in spring, the Roman troops were advancing on the shore in the direction of Perusium (Perugia) where the Carthaginians were supposed to be. The lake's level was then somewhat higher than it is today, so that only a narrow strip between its bank and the low hills near the present towns of Tuoro and Passignano remained. On a road built by either the Umbrians or the Etruscans the legions of Flaminius were proceeding in a widely extended marching formation when suddenly, out of the fog, the enemy, having lain in wait on the hills, pounced on them from three sides.

Hannibal's African contingent took on the Roman vanguard

while his other forces attacked the bulk and rear of the Roman columns. Many of the legionnaires who were not slaughtered were driven into the lake and drowned, weighed down by their armor and weapons. In the confusion, Flaminius himself was slain by a detachment of Gauls. Some six thousand Romans fought their way up to the hillsides, and only then, as the fog lifted, realized the magnitude of the catastrophe. They and other thousands of straggling legionnaires were taken prisoner, while some others managed to disperse into the countryside. The cry in Rome was *Hannibal ante portas!* (Hannibal is at our gates!).

Yet after his brilliant victory the Carthaginian didn't march on Rome as he might have done. Instead, he attempted to win new allies first. Among the Umbrian cities, Perusium and Spoleto remained loyal to Rome, but Todi and maybe Spello too opened their gates to the invaders. Hannibal eventually marched from Umbria to Apulia in Italy's deep south where, in 216 B.C., he inflicted another tremendous defeat on the Romans at Cannae. Rome did not give up. New legions were recruited and trained, Roman generals wore down the Carthaginian forces in Italy and North Africa, the fortunes of war turned, and Hannibal eventually committed suicide. Seventy years after the desperate day on Lake Trasimeno the city of Carthage was razed, and Rome was the world power it would remain for half a millennium.

Place names between Cortona and Tuoro, such as Sanguineto, Macerone, Ossaia, and Sepoltaia, refer to blood, massacres, bones, and graves. Even today, laborers turning the earth near the lake occasionally dig up a Roman spear, sword or helmet, or a skeleton that may be the remains of a Roman or Cathaginian soldier.

Tuoro, rising on the hillside like the tiers of an amphitheater looking down on the lake, also saw plenty of fighting in the late

Middle Ages and the Renaissance when feuding factions from Perugia and Arezzo clashed here. For centuries the town, situated as it was between the papal domains and the state of Tuscany, was a lair of smugglers and bandits. A hamlet a little to the west of Tuoro is called Dogana (Customs Station).

Camping sites are today spread along the lake. Some guests living in their trailers or under their tents stay considerably longer than do the migratory birds. One grassy plot on the lake shore is known as the Campo del Sole, or Sun Field. Thirty columns sculpted from soft, gray stone by modern Italian and foreign artists rise in this public space, each shaped differently, suggesting animal or plant motifs or displaying abstract patterns.

Tuoro and the bigger town of Passignano, four miles to the east, form the center of the so-called Umbrian Riviera. Its beaches, marinas, hotels, cafés, and discotheques attract visitors, especially on summer weekends, from all over the region and from adjoining Tuscany.

Passignano is a walled, old town on a hill with a vast, modern section on the beach, its "Lido." It is the principal vacation spot and harbor on the lake, with a small boat-building yard. Many Perugians keep their big or little lake craft moored here. The Isola Maggiore and Isola Minore, two of the three islands of Lake Trasimeno, look like one from the Passignano waterfront. Boat service links Passignano with the islands and with other towns around the lake. Signs at the approaches to Tuoro, Passignano, and other towns around here proclaim them as "denuclearized" communities. This is supposed to mean that their residents don't want any nuclear installations, civil or military, on their territory or in their surroundings, although there never were any in this part of the nation.

The green Isola Maggiore (Major Island), two miles from Passignano and more than a mile off Tuoro, seems to float serenely on the water, which is very clean in this area. Dense groves of pines and cypresses cover much of the island's twenty-seven acres. Its old fishermen's village, which a couple of generations ago counted some five hundred people, is now sparsely inhabited and eerily quiet after the day's last boat has left. Once, lace-making was a cottage industry on the Isola Maggiore; now shoreside plants with computer-piloted machinery supply the tourist market. The crenellated Villa Isabella at the island's southeastern tip, originally a monastery, is now a privately owned mansion. The highest point of the island, 150 feet above the lake, is crowned with a frescoed Gothic chapel; from the space in front of it one enjoys an enchanting panorama of the lake and its wreath of hills, especially on clear afternoons.

St. Francis of Assisi, according to legend (*Fioretti*, VII) spent forty-two days on the island, praying and fasting. The pious tale narrates that he had himself rowed by a boatman to Isola Maggiore, then uninhabited, on Ash Wednesday, February 16, 1211, carrying with him only two loaves of bread. Two chapels, one on the shore and the other on a nearby cliff, mark today the spots where the saint is said to have gone on land and where he built himself a little hut with tree branches and stones. When the boatman, as instructed, returned on Maundy Thursday (March 30) to take St. Francis back ashore, he found to his amazement that the penitent had eaten only half a loaf, leaving the remainder of the stale bread untouched. Today visitors to Isola Maggiore don't have to fast; there is a trattoria on the island, which also rents rooms.

The twelve-acre Isola Minore is also forested, but uninhabited today. The Isola Polvese, with an area of 133 acres, one mile off the eastern shore of the lake, is mostly flat. With its olive groves, rows of poplars, and other trees, the largest of the three islands is a favorite with hikers, campers, and wilderness lovers, but hardly anybody lives on it for lengthy periods.

⌁ Youth in a Very Old City ⌁

From the eastern shore of Lake Trasimeno it is only twelve miles to Perugia, Umbria's regional capital. Both the superhighway and the railroad line pass through several tunnels, with surprising vistas at their exits. Among other things, the traveler gets tantalizing glimpses of two medieval castles, Magione and Corciano.

The name Magione has the same Latin root as the English "mansion"; the brown hillside structure with its towers and walls, romantically surrounded by pines and cypresses, was originally a hostel for pilgrims who chose the route of Lake Trasimeno, which could be crossed by boat, for their arduous journey to or from Rome. The place was managed by the Knights Templar (who cared for such devout and tired travelers) in the thirteenth century, and later was taken over by a similar semimilitary confraternity, the Knights of Malta. Because of its strategic position, aristocratic clans in the neighborhood eventually coveted the hostel, acquired it, and fortified the complex. It is today one of the most impressive and attractive Renaissance castles in all of Umbria, the ideal setting for a costume movie. The stronghold changed hands several times, and over the centuries of a checkered history housed local warlords and visiting cardinals and popes.

Corciano, also a walled structure with a massive tower on a hill, was repeatedly besieged, at times withstanding the enemies, at others surrendering. The old hamlet around it, with a steep stairway leading up to the castle, is picturesque, but lately has sprawled with many new constructions at its feet, and is now virtually a suburb of the regional capital. Many industrial plants and workshops and ugly low-rent houses have gone up in the neighborhood, only three miles northwest of Perugia proper.

Last time I came through the town of Corciano it just happened to have drawn national attention to itself, and there was a lot of talk about such sudden and unwanted publicity in the coffee shop where I had an espresso.

The aromatic beverage in fact was the reason why many Italians for the first time heard of Corciano. Months earlier the mayor of the town had fired an employee, a municipal surveyor, on the ground that he had one time too often slipped out of the office to energize himself with espresso. The dismissed surveyor appealed for reinstatement to the Regional Administrative Tribunal (TAR) in Perugia, and the court upheld him. The official motivation for TAR's verdict was greeted with amusement and overwhelming approval all over the nation: A midmorning coffee break of, say, ten minutes is a time-honored Italian custom, TAR declared; an employee could be disciplined or dismissed only if the espresso absences during office hours were too long or too frequent. It may be added that in Rome a long sequence of new-broom chiefs of government departments have for decades been waging unsuccessful crusades against civil servants who spin out their hallowed coffee breaks into hour-long shopping expeditions or romantic assignations.

"We aren't slaves!," triumphantly proclaimed one of the patrons of the Corciano coffee shop as she dipped her *cornetto* (croissant) into her cappuccino. Probably she was taking time out of office duty, but I didn't ask her.

Approaching Perugia, the first-time visitor will be surprised, maybe even shocked, to see a clutter of modern residential and office buildings, hotels, high-rises, factories, storehouses, and service stations. Is that jumble supposed to generate the vaunted charm of the quaint Umbrian hill towns? But wait. Ascend from the broad twentieth-century belt around Perugia to find a very ancient urban core of impressive architectural integrity and timeless scenic beauty.

Perugia, unmistakably prosperous, has during the last several decades unstoppably expanded from its historic center 600 feet above its network of rail lines and highways and 1,000 feet above the Tiber Valley to its east; the city now counts 144,000 residents. From its hill and from the four major spurs branching out from it, Perugia has long spilled into the valleys around it.

The traveler arriving by car on winding access roads cannot normally get higher than the vast parking lot in the Piazzale Europa or the parking garage below the Piazza dei Partigiani. Motor traffic in the upper sections of the city is restricted. A system of underground escalators links the Piazza dei Partigiani (Partisans' Square), which looks out on a sports ground and on the Tiber Valley deep down, with the central Piazza d'Italia, one of the highest points of the city. The free ride on a series of escalators provides a chance for a good look at the bowels of the awesome Citadel that Pope Paul III had built in the sixteenth century. It is called the Rocca Paolina, and suggests Piranesi's *Prigioni*, his plates of imaginary, sinister prisons, engraved in 1750.

Perugia's main railroad station is at the foot of the old town's southern side, and passengers who won't climb on foot at least as far as the escalator near the Piazza dei Partigiani will have to take a cab or a public bus. An alternative is to get out of one's train at the station of Perugia-Ponte San Giovanni in the city's major industrial section near the Tiber on its southeastern side, and change into a local train that goes up to the Sant'Anna Station off the Piazza dei Partigiani. Long-distance buses running between Perugia and Rome, Florence, Gubbio, and other central Italian cities park in the Piazza dei Partigiani.

Old Perugia is all up and down, some sloping lanes actually being stairways with low steps. There are also more demanding stairs that may leave you breathless—literally, not figuratively. The reward for the continual exertions are marvelous vistas opening surprisingly at almost every turn. The parapet in the public park south of the Piazza d'Italia, behind the government building (the Prefecture), reveals to you the entire Umbrian Valley with Assisi, Spello, Foligno, Trevi, and other towns and villages. The panorama is best just before sunset when the hilly landscape is bathed in golden light. From other vantage points one not only may look far into the plains and at the hillsides of Umbria, but also may spy little gardens in the foreground where a few palm trees will grow—rather surprisingly in Perugia's climate.

Winters are cold and frequently bring snow, messing up traffic in the hilly neighborhoods. Between June and August temperatures of 100 degrees Fahrenheit and even hotter are no rarity. Spring and autumn are the best times for a visit.

Whoever comes to Perugia will at once notice that young people, including many non-Italians, are everywhere—at the rail station and the bus terminal, and in the historic center with its many espresso bars, pizzerie, taverns, and the faux-British beer pubs that have lately sprung up. Perugia State University is attended by tens of thousands of students not only from Umbria but also from other parts of the nation, especially from its south. They seek degrees in law, letters, biology, medicine, engineering, or architecture; Perugia has also one of Italy's few veterinarian schools. Furthermore, the city is since 1926 the seat of an Italian University for Foreigners; it occupies an eighteenth-century palazzo near one of Perugia's major landmarks, the massive Etruscan Arch. Subjects taught are Italian language, history, art and culture, and Etruscology (what little is known about the people who, more than 2,500 years ago, colonized Umbria).

Some of the students at the Foreigners' University are Americans who, having failed to win admission to a medical school at home, decided to earn a doctor's degree in Italy. Before being able to enroll in one of the country's medical schools they have to prove a measure of proficiency in the Italian language, which they acquire in Perugia. (An Italian-graduated M.D. cannot practice in the United States, not even as an intern; new exams at home would be required.)

Most of the several thousand students at the Foreigners' University are from developing countries, admitted into Italy on student visas. Quite a few of them have won scholarships, and are expected eventually to return home to put their new knowledge and skills at the service of their own people. However, as elsewhere, the graduates often attempt to stay on in the host country, or to immigrate to some other advanced nation. The Italian police and secret services keep watching the vast Perugia youth scene with special attention, always suspecting that at least a few pre-

sumed foreign students are involved in radical or possibly terror-
ist networks, or are implicated in the drug traffic which, alas, is
rampant in the city.

Since there is no on-campus accommodation in Perugia, out-
of-town Italian students and their foreign companions live either
in one of the few hostels—most of them church-run—or in rented rooms and apartments. Providing shelter for students is a
Perugia industry. I know a well-to-do real estate owner in Spoleto
who has bought and summarily fixed up several apartments in
Perugia as an investment, renting them out to groups of youngsters who share them. The landlord comes to town from time to
time to collect rents; look after his properties; and have the
wiring, plumbing, and locks repaired and lightbulbs replaced
whenever necessary. He admits he prefers to rent to students
rather than to other people because he easily gets them evicted if
they don't pay or if he doesn't like them, whereas older tenants,
especially Italian families, would invoke rent control and put up a
legal fight if he wanted to get them out.

My friend Guillaume is a Rwandan who was sent to Perugia on
a grant from his government. Being brought up in French at home
in Kigali, he had first to learn Italian, and then he started working
for an Italian law degree at Perugia University. What can you do
with it in Rwanda? I asked him several times. "Oh, the important
thing in law is to know the general principles and mechanisms,"
he used to explain. "One then quickly learns the juridical system
of a given country." Living in a church-affiliated student hostel,
Guillaume was preparing his dissertation on a point of international law when he learned that his father, a Hutu justice of the
Rwandan High Court, had been slain by Tutsis; his mother and
two sisters had managed to flee to Belgium. Guillaume doggedly

completed his studies, graduated with distinction, and to Italians was a *dottore*. He might have found some job in Italy, but he wished to go home—"I don't want to be a black in a white country all my life." He conceded he hadn't experienced blatant discrimination in Perugia, but had never felt quite comfortable either.

His local friends and I urged Guillaume to postpone plans for returning to Africa until the still smoldering conflict between Hutus and Tutsis in Rwanda subsided. The Italian authorities prolonged his visa but told him that eventually he must leave. We urged him to apply for political asylum, which would have enabled him to stay on indefinitely and earn his upkeep. Understandably, Guillaume wanted to see his mother and sisters in Belgium, but that country, once the colonial power in Rwanda, wouldn't give him a visa for even a short reunion with the survivors of his family. Despite our misgivings, the Rwandan *dottore* eventually flew to Kigali. Later we heard he had been hired by the Rwandan foreign ministry.

Such case histories aren't rare in the Umbrian capital. With its many thousand Italian and foreign students and hundreds of academic teachers, Perugia boasts the liveliest intellectual and artistic life in the entire region, and offers more cultural events and opportunities than do much bigger Italian cities.

Official and private promoters during the last few years thought up periodic affairs that are supposed to enhance Perugia's reputation as a cultural center and, not incidentally, to attract more tourists. A youth festival in June is called "Rockin' Umbria," and a similar musical parade in the middle of July is known as "Jazz Umbria."

A platform goes up in the Piazza della Repubblica for the performers, and electronic systems fill the square and the neighborhoods around it with sound until late at night. The troupe of Perugia's Teatro Morlacchi—named after a native son, the nineteenth-century conductor and composer Francesco Morlacchi—stages outdoor shows in July and August. In August and September musical bands from all over Umbria play in open-air concerts, and at the end of October an antiques and jewelry fair is held in the city.

A literature student from Foligno had this to say about her university years in Perugia: "I can go to a play, a concert by a visiting soloist or group, or to a movie revival almost every day. It's not so sleepy here as it is at home. In Foligno, television and, on the weekend, the discotheque are about everything, and people speak mostly about soccer."

Not that Perugia isn't gripped by sports fever too when its own soccer team faces one of its historic adversaries, like the Terni eleven. Whenever there is a home match, police reinforcements are moved into the city to protect the visiting players and, especially, the referee. Soccer madness reached a peak in June 1996 when the Perugia Football Club, in a crucial home event, defeated Verona, from the far north, three to two, qualifying again for the first division of the national soccer league. The Perugia had languished in the second division for the last fifteen years, and the team's return to the top group of Italy's rich, professional soccer set off delirium in the city. The crackle and booms of powerful firecrackers could be heard for hours, flags in the Perugia club's white and red appeared in many windows, and thousands of celebrating fans roamed the streets and squares of the center all night. When I arrived in Perugia on one of my periodic visits three days later, the flags were still fluttering everywhere and people talked about little else besides the soccer triumph.

Even one of Perugia's best-known street characters acknowledged the local team's success, though in his own bizarre way. A middle-aged Umbrian, he is a militant supporter of the first-division club Juventus of Turin, in Italy's relatively remote northwest. For years he had walked around the center of Perugia, perversely and provokingly sporting the black-and-white-striped shirt of the Juventus players almost every day. Local people had long given up taunting him, also because the lone Juventus fan was apt to explode in abuse if vexed. Whenever he inveighed at someone incautious enough to make fun of him or the Juventus, his accent betrayed him as a genuine native of the region, not a northerner. After the apotheosis of the Perugia Football Club, the Juventus enthusiast left his black-and-white shirt at home, at least for a few days, and strutted around the city core in a fancy military uniform, apparently of his own design.

∿ The Language of Stones ∿

Perugia is at least 2,500 years old. Umbrians had been living on its hill for hundreds of years when Etruscans conquered it in the sixth or fifth century B.C. and pushed Umbrian clans east of the Tiber; many of the humbler people probably remained where they had been tilling their fields, raising their cattle, and plying their trades. The new overlords erected sturdy city walls from around 400 B.C. when Celtic raiders (whom the Romans called Gauls) repeatedly swept into Italy from the north.

In 390 B.C. a band of Celtic warriors led by one Brennus penetrated as far south as Rome, defeated the Roman army, sacked the city, and laid siege to the capital. Livy's famous anecdote (which isn't necessarily accurate) has a dispute over the weight of ransom gold arising as the withdrawal of the Gauls with their plunder is being negotiated, and Brennus throwing his sword into the scales with the terrible words *Vae victis!* (Woe to the vanquished!) In Etruscan Perugia, at the time, there would have been much more to loot than in comparatively primitive Rome, and it stands to reason that the wealthy city earnestly thought about improving its defenses.

The Etruscan walls around the crown of the hill, now the city core, were a little less than two miles in circumference. Long stretches of them can still be seen or traced today, especially in the west and southwest of old Perugia. Scholars assume that at the peak of the Etruscan city's prosperity as many as forty thousand people lived in it, that population undoubtedly including many Umbrian laborers and slaves. Most of what we know about Etruscan Perugia is what its stones tell us.

A particularly impressive section of the pre-Roman fortifications is the Etruscan Arch to the north. When it was erected in the fourth century B.C., it was the main gate of the city, and over two millennia it has become something like a quick summary of Perugian history. The lower part of the arched gateway and the two towers flanking it, rugged like Apennine rocks, are solid, time-defying Etruscan work. Rectangularly cut stone blocks are heaped on one another, mostly without mortar, conveying a sense of enormous strength.

Looking at the massive semicircular vault, one is reminded that it was the Etruscans who developed the arch, which they had copied from oriental and Greek models into an important element of their construction idiom, and that they taught it to the Romans. The Etruscan Arch of Perugia is cited in architecture textbooks as a prototype. Gifted disciples of their Etruscan masters, the Roman architects would make the arch, in combination with columns, into the principal feature of their buildings, using it not only for religious and mundane constructions, but also for monumental purposes as free-standing triumphal arches.

Etruscan are also the stylized decorations inside the vaults of the gate and the motif of five round stone shields between short columns above it. The Romans, who conquered Perugia in 310 B.C., used the stout arch the way it had served under the Etruscans, as the principal city gate. It was damaged, and the city was half-destroyed, when Perugia became a pawn in the civil war between Mark Anthony and Octavian (who was soon to be known as Augustus) in 41–40 B.C. Under Augustus the city was rebuilt and the Etruscan Gate repaired; the old Etruscan-Latin name of the city was officially twinned with that of the empire's new master, and the two words were inscribed on the old arch: AUGUSTA PERUSIA.

A short arch was put on top of the Etruscan Gate as a sentry box and lookout during the Roman imperial era, but walled up later. A graceful Renaissance loggia sitting on the left (north) tower of the gate and a marble fountain at its bottom were added in the early sixteenth century.

Another city gate going back to the Etruscans is the Porta Marzia (Mars Gate) below Piazza d'Italia. It once didn't stand on exactly that spot but nearby, and only the arch with its topmost decorations (whose meaning is obscure) survive. The architect Antonio da Sangallo the Younger had the remains respectfully dismantled when he needed the space for the Citadel he was constructing at the behest of Pope Paul III (p. 37), and had the gate rebuilt stone by stone, incorporating it into the wall of the new fortress.

A monumental Etruscan well can be visited in a house at 1 Piazza Piccinino, facing the Cathedral. It is not quite as deep as St. Patrick's Well in Orvieto, but it's nearly 2,000 years older. The Etruscan engineers not only dug many shafts and reservoirs, they also pierced the city's stony subsoil with drains and sewers; only a part of this subterranean maze has been explored so far.

A large part of Perugia's tangible Etruscan heritage, especially many objects found in tombs, can be viewed today in museums elsewhere in Italy and abroad. A number of important exhibits have fortunately been saved for Perugia's own National Archeological Museum. Famous among these is the Perugine Table, known to scholars as *Cippus Perusinus,* a travertine slab with one of the longest known inscriptions in the Etruscan language, found near the city in 1822. Its 45 lines with together 151 words were interpreted as a deed sealing the partition of land between two clans. The Etruscans must have had not only accomplished architects, sculptors, frescoists, dancers, musicians, jugglers, and soothsayers, but also skilled surveyors and sharp lawyers.

Other noteworthy Etruscan objects in the museum are sarcophagi, Egyptian finds from Etruscan tombs, toiletry articles, jewelry, bronzes, and vases. The overall impression is that of a refined civilization that was trading with Greece, Egypt, Cyprus, and the Phoenicians when Rome was barely stirring. The Roman sculptures and other artifacts in the collection are unexceptional.

During the long Roman domination Perugia appears to have enjoyed a quiet, affluent life, brutally interrupted only by the horrors of the civil war after Caesar's assassination. Curiously, no amphitheater or arena has been found up to now in or near ancient Perugia, whereas such Umbrian towns as Gubbio or Spello, which are today much smaller than the regional capital, have well-preserved ruins of such structures, which in the Roman Empire meant as much for the self-esteem of provincials as cathedrals would mean in the Middle Ages and Olympic-class sports facilities mean today.

◡⦂ Umbrian School ⦂◡

First-time visitors to Perugia who aren't particularly interested in antiquities and want to get an overall impression of the city will start sight-seeing in its very heart, Piazza Quattro Novembre. On its north side is the cathedral, built in the Gothic style between 1345 and 1490, and never quite finished. Externally, naked gray-brown brick walls are showing, although one section, facing the main square, is covered with white and red marble in a geometric pattern. Local youngsters, visiting school classes from other parts of Italy, and picnicking tourists often sit on the stairs leading up to the side entrance.

At the right side of that portal is a late-Gothic pulpit from which St. Bernardine of Siena, an austere and eloquent Franciscan, preached to a vast crowd of Perugians in 1425. Left of the side entrance is a seated bronze statue of Pope Julius III, executed by Vincenzo Danti, a local admirer of Michelangelo; the sculpture from the year 1455 was meant as a token of the city's gratitude for the restoration of some of its old privileges by the pontiff. Farther left is a Renaissance loggia..

The main portal of the cathedral, on Piazza Danti, is a Baroque sixteenth-century addition. The vast inside of the church contains a marble sarcophagus with the remains of two popes who died in Perugia, Urban IV (1264)—the Frenchman who started the Cathedral of Orvieto—and Martin IV (1285).

The north aisle, known as the Chapel of the Holy Ring, is closed by an iron gate; it owes its name to a revered trinket, believed to be the wedding band of the Virgin Mary, contained in a precious reliquary. The chapel was once adorned with Perugino's *Sposalizio*, depicting the wedding of Mary of Nazareth and Joseph (1503), which inspired Raphael's even more famous painting of the same theme and name (now in Milan's Brera Gallery). Napoleon had the Perugino work taken from the chapel during his Italian campaign in 1797, and had it sent to France with many other looted art treasures; the Perugino *Sposalizio* is today in Caen, Normandy.

The cathedral is adjoined by the large seminary, around an imposing courtyard. The stately building houses the Cathedral Museum, with an altarpiece by Luca Signorelli representing the Madonna, a Lute-Playing Angel and Saints (1484), other art, illuminated manuscripts, and liturgical objects. The west side of the Piazza Quattro Novembre is taken up by the Bishop's Palace, going back to the fourteenth century, in which several popes resided during their frequent sojourns in the city.

The Cathedral's left side faces, across the square, the Gothic, battlemented Palazzo dei Priori (Palace of Civic Leaders), the medieval city hall. This proud edifice was built in sections between 1293 and 1443; it is remarkable for its bulk and for its fine windows, each with three openings. A fanlike flight of stairs leads up to a splendid portal; above it are a bronze griffin, the heraldic animal of Perugia, and a lion, symbolizing the papal (Guelph) party with which Perugia used to align itself. The emblematic animals triumphantly hold up the chains and bars of another city's gates—trophies of a victory that Perugia won over Siena, an old rival, in 1358. At the right side of the portal is the remnant of an outer pulpit from which officials would read municipal decrees to the citizenry. The upper floor of the palace is occupied by the National Gallery of Umbria (p. 50).

At the center of the Piazza Quattro Novembre is the Fontana Maggiore (Major Fountain), from the thirteenth century, which is fed by an aqueduct. The elegant composition consists of three basins of different diameters—two of marble and one of bronze—one above the other, decorated with small columns and high-relief figures of biblical characters and of allegorical personages representing the arts and the months of the year. The fountain is the work mainly of two renowned sculptors from Pisa, Niccolo and Giovanni Pisano. It is today protected from vandals by an iron fence around the first of the five circular steps leading up to the largest and lowest of the three basins.

The visitor who sits on the cathedral steps and looks at the attractively dignified piazza with its playing children, strolling Perugians and tourists, and the people spooning gelato or sipping cappuccino at the café tables to the left is likely to experience a sense of serenity—a feeling bound to deepen if one walks a few hundred yards to one of several vantage points for gazing into the gentle Umbrian landscape. One finds it hard to believe that this square and this city could have been the scene of unspeakable violence and crimes in the Middle Ages and the Renaissance.

Yet the chronicles tell of horrors in the almost uninterrupted feuds the city had to endure. Above all, two aristocratic clans, the Baglioni and the Oddi, kept fighting for control of Perugia over several generations. There were massacres, popular tumults, poison plots, sensational assassinations, spectacular vendettas, and multiple public hangings. At one time the Baglioni used even the cathedral as their military barracks.

From time to time the clergy called for penitential processions and public prayers to atone for the savagery, but enmities would soon flare up again. The year 1348 was particularly sinister: A famine was followed by the black plague, which filled mass graves to overflowing, and in the autumn of that year a violent earthquake caused many houses to collapse, killed a great number of Perugians, and toppled the upper two basins of the Fontana Maggiore. In 1491 thirty-five altars were erected in the ominous square, and for three days masses were said to implore heavenly forgiveness for the latest wave of atrocities in the city.

It is one of the miracles of Umbria that during such times of nearly seamless violence, outstanding masters should have created art of moving tenderness and deep mysticism. To view an important cross-section of the Umbrian School of painting, walk the few steps from the central square to the main entrance of the Palazzo dei Priori on Corso Vannucci. That principal street is named after Pietro Vannucci, the greatest Umbrian painter and Raphael's teacher, who is known by the name of the city where he did much of the work in his mature years. The National Gallery of Umbria on the fourth floor of the Palazzo dei Priori was originally called the Vannucci Gallery; it is the foremost collection of Umbrian art, although many works by the astonishingly productive Perugino and of other Umbrian painters are today treasured by museums and collections all over the world.

The State Gallery in Perugia vaunts such major Perugino paintings as the *Adoration of the Magi* and several Madonnas. There are also many works by that other great Umbrian, Pinturicchio (or Pintoricchio), the "little painter" (1454–1513), whose real name was Bernardino di Betto, and by disciples of Perugino—but not by Raphael, who was an assistant in Perugino's workshop from 1499 to 1503. Many masters from Siena and other Tuscans, like Fra Angelico, are represented by significant works. They include a priceless panel composition by Piero della Francesca representing the Madonna with Four Saints and the Annunciation.

Visitors to the Palazzo dei Priori may also see the Historical Collection of the City and Territory of Perugia, with plans of the old fortifications, as well as the second-floor Hall of the Notaries, adorned with the coats of arms of former dignitaries, frescoes of biblical and allegorical scenes, and seventeenth-century wooden stalls.

Next door to the Palazzo dei Priori on the Corso Vannucci is the old money exchange, Collegio del Cambio, which Perugino frescoed between 1498 and 1507 for a fee of 350 ducats. His assistants, among whom was possibly the young Raphael, helped him in this undertaking in the rectangular, vaulted main hall (Sala dell'Udienza del Cambio). The stateliness of the 500-year-old office of the money changers may surprise in an era of credit cards and electronic teller machines; currency transactions in the Renaissance with their many big and small states that struck coins, and with renowned banking houses that issued letters of credit, were matters of paramount importance and great complexity.

The best light for viewing the pictures of the Collegio del Cambio is between eleven A.M. and twelve noon. The frescoes form a cycle that, in a characteristic Renaissance vein, mixes pagan divinities with biblical personages, and the sages of classical antiquity with angels and prophets. Perugino painted his self-portrait on the pillar between the two vaults; it shows him as a corpulent, placid-looking man wearing a red cap over flowing, chestnut-colored hair, who is raising his eyebrows as he gazes at the canvas. It has long been a guessing game among art historians as to which—if any—figures the seventeen-year-old Raphael was allowed to paint, and whether he smuggled his own likeness into the tableaux. Perugino's most loyal assistant, Giannicola di Paolo Manni, at the time much more esteemed than was the relative novice Raphael, contributed an altarpiece and frescoes to the chapel of the money changers' guild, adjacent to the principal hall.

⌁ The Shuffle ⌁

It is doubtful whether Perugino, relaxed though he looks in his self-portrait, found much time for strolling in the main street that was to be named for him long after his death. The Perugians then very likely already sauntered up and down in front of the money changers' center whenever mayhem in the streets didn't make it advisable to stay indoors. The busy master from Città della Pieve had received his early training in Florence and other places in Tuscany, had worked in the Vatican and was widely known outside Umbria; commissions poured in, and Perugino didn't like to turn down any of them. He was notoriously fond of money, or maybe his wife Chiara was (her face is said to have been that of many of his Madonnas).

Today, as in the calmer spells of the Renaissance age, the leisurely stroll along the three hundred yards of the Corso Vannucci is a daily or twice-daily ritual for many people: the *passeggio* (promenade) or *struscio* (shuffle). Every day around noon and again in the late afternoon hundreds will walk up and down the corso, and once again up and down, between the Piazza Quattro Novembre and the square at its western end, the Piazza d'Italia. They look at the shop windows, maybe stop for an espresso, say hello to acquaintances, chat with a friend, possibly flirt a little with a prospective partner in a future affair. Nothing, of course, goes unobserved, because most people know one another at least by sight. Returning to Perugia every now and then, I see many seemingly perennial characters of the daily outdoor comedy that is the *struscio*. One of them is the Juventus diehard in his black-and-white soccer shirt, which was briefly replaced by his fantasy military uniform.

The rectangular Piazza d'Italia with cedar trees transplanted from the Lebanon in a park and a monument of King Victor Emmanuel II in its middle is the nerve center of Umbria. On its south side is the Prefecture building, erected after Italy's unification in 1870; it is the seat of the provincial administration, which represents the central government in Rome. From the windows the officials can overlook much of the territory that they supervise.

At the rear side of the Prefecture is a small park with a monument of Perugino, put up there in 1923. There is also a bust of the poet Giosuè Carducci (1835–1907), the Tuscan professor of literature who as a government-appointed school inspector repeatedly toured Umbria, which inspired him to write verses about various aspects of the region. The view from the parapet behind the Prefecture is famous (p. 38).

An escalator on the right (west) side of the Prefecture is a link of the people-moving system that provides a connection between the city center and the bus terminal and other lower-lying neighborhoods. Descending, the visitor at once gets an almost oppressive sense of the Citadel, the Rocca Paolina (p. 37) that Pope Paul III had constructed *ad repellendam Perusinorum audaciam* (to repel the temerity of the Perugians), as he took care to explain in an inscription. The hated papal fortress was devastated in a revolt in 1848, and most of it was razed after Italy's unification. Some underground chambers that survived the demolition are used today for art shows.

Opposite the Prefecture in the Piazza d'Italia stands a building in which the offices of the Region of Umbria are now ensconced. They were created after 1970 when the old territorial units of Italy, which in the unified nation until then had possessed merely geographical and historic significance, attained a measure of self-government.

Umbria comprises the provinces of Perugia and Terni, and the new regional machinery was an additional bureaucratic tier inserted between City Hall (which has offices in the Palazzo dei Priori and in locations around town) and the central government in Rome with its Prefecture outposts in the cities of Perugia and Terni. Perugia's new role, since 1970, as the regional capital brought more public funds to manage, more personnel to hire, and more opportunities for politicking and log-rolling to Umbria's biggest center. What's going on in the Regional Assembly and the Regional Government, and their bureaucratic and political sparring with City Hall and Rome, supplies plenty of topics for gossip during the twice-daily strolls in the Corso Vannucci.

The west side of the Piazza d'Italia is taken up by the regional branch of the Bank of Italy and by the Brufani Hotel. Although downsized to just two dozen rooms, this is still the leading establishment in which to stay. Giacomo Brufani, the nineteenth-century founder, was a boy from the Umbrian countryside whom a foreign painter took with him to Paris as a manservant. Young Brufani later worked there and in Milan, Rome, and London as a travel guide; he married an Englishwoman, Elizabeth Platt, and eventually opened in Perugia his own hotel, which he geared to British tastes. Ownership later passed into British hands; when I first was a guest at the Brufani for a couple of days in the early 1950s, the English tea ceremonial, scones and all, was still rigorously observed at five P.M. daily.

To me, one of the great Perugia pleasures is strolling at random in the ancient quarters. It's my own, private "shuffle" on narrow, possibly sloping lanes under arches and vaults (often one above the other in catercorner patterns of stones, masonry, light, and shade), climbing steep stairways and discovering picturesque corners or unexpected vistas that I had never seen before during my many visits.

A walk to Perugia's food market to pick up wine or cheese is a kaleidoscopic parade of history. From the central Piazza Quattro Novembre you descend by a short, sloping street, past the main post office, into another irregular square, Piazza Matteotti (named after the Socialist leader whom Fascist thugs murdered in 1924). In the middle of the square is a bronze statue of Garibaldi; the national hero was often in Umbria, but only briefly in Perugia, in 1848.

On the east side of the Piazza Matteotti stands the elongated, low Palazzo of the Captains of the People, built in soberly elegant Renaissance style, 1472–81, by Northern Italian architects. The Captain of the People, in Perugia as in other Umbrian cities, was the commander of the civic militia who, as a political counterweight to the mayor, often also had nonmilitary functions. Adjacent is the Old University, also erected in the fifteenth century. Today both edifices and a neighboring, more recent, building are occupied by the courts of law. Perugia State University now has its main campus on the northern outskirts.

A passageway near the Old University leads to a fourteenth-century loggia, from which one descends to a vast and well-ordered covered market on a terrace built in the 1930s. The stands abound in fresh produce from the countryside. Walk to the edge of the market to see forty-five-foot-tall pillars resting on the substructures of the Etruscan town walls to support the Palace of the Captain of the People and the nearby buildings. The Piazza Matteotti, in fact, is also known as the Piazza del Sopramuro (Square Above the Wall). A public elevator links piazza and market with the low-lying neighborhoods outside the ancient walls.

Or stroll from the north side of Piazza Matteotti through twisting streets to what has remained of the ancient Church of San Severo (which is said to have been built soon after the year 1000 over the ruins of a pagan temple of the sun god). A surviving rectangular chapel contains a restored fresco by the twenty-two-year-old Raphael, one of his first independent works. Raphael had left Perugino's shop and gone to Florence, but returned to Perugia in 1505 to decorate the chapel of what was then a monastery. The part of the fresco that has been saved from decay shows Jesus between two angels and six sainted Camaldolese monks who were martyred in Poland in 1003. Art historians point out that the work demonstrates how the young Raphael, newly influenced by Tuscan art, transcended the Umbrian School. Figures of saints, lower at the sides, were painted by the aged Perugino in 1521, the year after his most famous pupil's death.

West of the Corso Vannucci, walk under the vaulted passage below the municipal clock tower down the steep Via dei Priori. A city map may be needed to find the small Via Deliziosa, starting from the left side of that street, where a tablet at No. 5 marks the presumed house of Perugino.

Continuing downward on the Via dei Priori, past the small Renaissance church of the Madonna della Luce (Madonna of the Light), the stroller reaches the magnificent fifteenth-century facade of the Oratory of St. Bernardine. Its numerous sculptures and low reliefs in colored marble and terra-cotta on pastel-hued ground are the work of the Florentine sculptor Agostino d'Antonio di Duccio, 1457–61. The oratory, or chapel, was built in honor of the sainted Franciscan preacher from Siena (p. 47), who during his several visits to Perugia always stayed at the near-by Franciscan convent, at present the seat of the Academy of Fine Arts, with a small museum.

A longer stroll or a car ride for two thirds of a mile in the oppo-site direction on the much-traveled Corso Cavour to the Church of San Pietro on Perugia's southeastern spur is a must. The visitor passes a double city gate, Porta San Pietro or Porta Romana (Roman Gate); the inner arch is from the fourteenth century, the elegant outer doorway was designed by Agostino di Duccio, who created the facade of St. Bernardine's.

St. Peter's, 400 yards beyond that Renaissance gate, is a vast complex of buildings that today includes the Agricultural University. The slim, octagonal, fifteenth-century steeple of the church, with a high octagonal pyramid on top, is visible from many points in the city and its surroundings and is a striking fea-ture of Perugia's skyline. The slopes of the spur carrying St. Peter's are covered with olive groves.

I had seen the cluster of old edifices and the works of art in them much earlier, but recently I walked out to it again with a friend who was a newcomer to Perugia. We lingered a little in the park in front of the church, admiring the view of the countryside below. When we approached St. Peter's we were stopped by an elderly man in a black cassock—a friar or a priest?—who seemed to be waiting for somebody. "Want to see the church?" he asked. "I'll show it to you." I had the impression he hadn't anything better to do, and maybe was bored, and said we'd be glad to be guided by him. It turned out to be a good move because he had the key to the sacristy, which contains major art treasures. I eventually realized that our mentor was the guardian or sacristan of the church, and had simply been on the lookout for sightseers, rare in the off-season period (it was January). He may have been some kind of ecclesiastic, though.

Leading us into the church he started a well-practiced spiel. He explained that the edifice was erected in the tenth century on the spot where Perugia's first cathedral (or bishop's see) had been standing. Of course, our guide said, the church over the centuries was often repaired, altered, and embellished. "Look at those granite and marble columns," he ordered. "They are from antiquity; most are Ionic, but two are Corinthian. They probably belonged to some pagan temple. They were put up in the tenth century, but the flat ceiling they carry is from the sixteenth century." Then he pointed out the paintings and frescoes on the walls of the nave, the transept, and the vaulted aisles. There were large canvases by a pupil of Tintoretto, copies of Raphael paintings, and pictures by minor Umbrian artists whose names I had never heard before and quickly forgot.

The sacristy, unlocked by our guide, is actually a large chapel. We were shown paintings of saints by Perugino, a St. Francesca Romana with an Angel that is attributed to Caravaggio (but may be by a disciple), and other Renaissance and Baroque works of art. The guide let us into the choir and claimed that its carved and inlaid walnut-wood stalls from the sixteenth century were the most beautiful in all of Italy; we wouldn't dispute him. A graffito in the choir reads: "Giosuè Carducci, 7 Sept. 1877." It is anybody's guess whether the inscription was scrawled by the poet (p. 53) himself or by someone who usurped his name. Eventually our guide opened a little door in the apse and told us to step out on a narrow balcony that seemed suspended in the air. This *loggetta* commands an extraordinary panorama of the Umbrian Valley and the hills as far east as Montefalco and Spello. "You should have come toward evening," the guide said. "You might have seen high mountain peaks on the horizon."

I put a folded 10,000 lire note (around $6 at the time) in our guide's palm and, uncertain whether he was a clergyman or the sacristan, mumbled that the money was for "your charities." He put the banknote in the pocket of his cassock, thanked with dignity, and said we could visit the courtyards of the Agricultural University on our own; they were former cloisters of what had once been a Benedictine monastery and deserved to be seen. Future agronomists, including a few women students, were milling about in the two courtyards, one from the fifteenth century and one from the sixteenth, both of noble architecture.

✌ *Tombs, Oil, and Wine* ✢

If we had come by car to St. Peter's, we might have proceeded for another two miles or so to the famous Tomb of the Volumnii. I had visited this elaborate burial place of an aristocratic and wealthy Etruscan family twice earlier, and either time was more deeply impressed by it than I had been by the Etruscan cemeteries of Cerveteri north of Rome, and of Orvieto.

The Volumnii Tomb is from the second century B.C. when

Etruscan power in Perugia and elsewhere had long been broken, but the religious and cultural traditions of the former overlords were still alive in Umbria. A farmer discovered the burial site in February 1840 while he was plowing, when his ox suddenly sank into what seemed a cave. The grave chambers, cut into the tufa below the topsoil, are now a major sight-seeing attraction, known as the Ipogeo, which is Italian for hypogeum, or catacomb. The little modern building above the excavations contains a collection of Etruscan artifacts found here and in other burial sites around Perugia—bronze and terra-cotta objects, some adorned with relief sculptures showing scenes of Etruscan and Greek mythology; and sculpted winged monsters that suggest the fabulous griffin that has been Perugia's own totem since time immemorial.

A flight of twenty-nine steep, ancient steps descends to the entrance, which is adorned with a carved shield between two dolphins. Today the underground complex has electric lighting; the original bronze hooks for torches or oil lamps are still visible. The tomb has the layout of an ancient Etruscan or Roman house with nine chambers and other cell-like openings around an oblong space, the atrium. This rectangular room is covered with what seems a double sloping roof with simulated beams carved out of the tufa. One chamber contains nine funerary chests made of travertine, the largest showing in sculptures the dead family chief resting on a bed, supported by two winged genii of death. An Etruscan inscription identifies the dead man as Arnth Valimnas Aules, which scholars have translated as Arunte Volumnius, son of Aulus. He is believed to have been a magistrate, and presumably was rich and influential. Left of Arunte's urn is that of his daughter Velia, under a statue showing her solemnly sitting on a matron's chair.

There is also a chest from a latter period when the Romans must already have been firmly in power; it holds the pulverized remains of one Publius Volumnius Aulus, possibly the last of the Etruscan clan of the Volumnii. After his burial the tomb was probably soon forgotten, and the entrance to it filled up with wind-blown earth.

In both of my visits to the Ipogeo I imagined how gloomy it must have looked when it was illuminated by dim oil lamps instead of by electricity. The second time a friend who was with me seemed relieved when we came up the twenty-nine steps from the Etruscan netherworld, and quoted Dante emerging with Virgil from the Inferno: "We came forth to see again the stars." Actually it was bright sunshine that we saw, suffusing the bucolic country-side. My friend remarked: "I wouldn't care to go down there at night, stars or no stars afterward."

Bucolic though the site of the Etruscan tomb may look, it is close to Perugia's industrial suburb Ponte San Giovanni, once a separate little town named after a Roman bridge across the Tiber. The original Ponte San Giovanni is believed to have been an Etruscan river port. Today, administratively belonging to Perugia, the suburb is a railroad and highway hub, and an agglomeration of workshops, commercial buildings, and modern residential developments. A railroad spur line climbs from Ponte San Giovanni station to Perugia's Sant'Anna Station (p. 38).

Five miles downstream, on the left (east) bank of the Tiber, where the Chiascio River joins it, the picturesque old wine town of Torgiano is perched on a little promontory. Vineyards cover the rolling countryside. Every now and then ancient amphorae (two-handled jars) are still dug up in some field or building site, proof that wine was grown, stored, and probably shipped here already in Etruscan-Roman times. Ancient tombs uncovered near the confluence of the two rivers have yielded vintners' equipment among other artifacts.

In 1974 the Lungarotti family of Torgiano, vintners for generations, opened a private wine museum, which continues to draw many visitors. It takes up twenty rooms in the seventeenth-century Palazzo Graziani Baglioni on the town's main street. The collection retraces the origin of viticulture in the Middle East and indicates the trade routes and sea lanes on which vine plants arrived in Mediterranean countries, including Italy. There are Hittite vases, pottery from the Cyclades connected with wine making, Etruscan bronzes, and ancient Roman amphorae.

A vaulted basement hall contains huge wooden wine presses. A medieval section illustrates the use of wine as food and as a medicine. Old books and prints as well as sculptures and drawings from the Renaissance to Picasso exemplify the importance of wine in myth, art, and popular culture. Also on display are samples of the tools once used by coopers, vat makers, innkeepers, and other wine trades. Exhibits on viticulture in Umbria and an enological library round out the museum, which is administered by the Lungarotti Foundation.

American friends of mine who had arrived in Perugia by train recently decided to visit the Lungarotti estate (which comprises also a hotel and a restaurant). They took the public bus for Torgiano at Perugia's Piazza dei Partigiani. They must have had a good time, sampling the wine, for they missed the return bus from nearby Bettona to Perugia, which was supposed to stop at Torgiano. It was getting dark, as they reported to me later, and they were a little worried. Soon, however, a car with PG (Perugia) license plates stopped, the driver asking, Is there a problem? My friends told him their predicament, he offered them a ride as he himself was bound for Perugia, and in a quarter of an hour they were back in the center of the city. I note this episode here because many Italian drivers, afraid of robbers and car jackers, have lately been reluctant to take unknown persons aboard; the authorities frown on hitchhiking (it is illegal on motorways). In Umbria one may still thumb a free ride.

Bettona, the small town three miles east of Torgiano, whence the rescuer of my American friends came, is renowned for one of the most charming panoramas in all of Umbria. From its hill 600 feet above the Cascio River the town looks out on sloping olive groves and green and yellow fields in the foreground, at distant Perugia on the left, and Assisi, Spello, and Foligno on the right.

A ruined castle tops a hill near Torgiano. High walls of sandstone blocks in an oval layout surround Bettona; they were started by the Etruscans when the originally Umbrian hill town, then called Vettona, became a colony of Etruscan Perugia. The fortifications were repeatedly repaired by the Romans and by medieval rulers. An elaborate Etruscan tomb from the fourth century B.C. is a few hundred yards outside the walls; tasteful jewelry found in it is now displayed in the National Museum of Villa Giulia in Rome.

Under the ancient Romans this was a flourishing town with a temple and a forum. Like other Umbrian places, Bettona suffered grievously during the barbarian invasions and from the wars between medieval factions; a Perugian force all but destroyed the town in the fourteenth century. The Baglioni party eventually won control, and on the main square built a Gothic palace with large windows, which today houses a small but interesting museum. Its picture collection includes several works by the prolific

Perugino and by other Umbrian masters; there are also some Etruscan objects in terra-cotta and bronze.

Bettona's panorama is particularly enchanting from a window in the sacristy of San Crispoldo's, a thirteenth-century church on a little piazza adjoining the main square. St. Crispoldo, according to legend, was a native of Jerusalem whom the Apostle Peter sent or called to Italy to preach the message of Jesus Christ. He is supposed to have come to Bettona, worked many miracles, became the town's first bishop, and suffered martyrdom under Emperor Maximian. If this pious story were true, St. Crispoldo would have lived at least 200 years, since Maximian, essentially a soldier, was subemperor and eventually emperor, A.D. 285–310. But maybe the first bishop of Bettona had received a heavenly command from the long-dead Prince of the Apostles. The fame of St. Crispoldo and his reputation as a miracle worker at any rate was so great that the Perugians took his remains to their own city in 1352 when they devastated Bettona. The relics of the saint were returned only in 1371, and since then they have rested in an urn in a chapel on the left side of his church. Umbrians have always been proud of their saints, and possessive with regard to their bones.

Visitors to Torgiano and Bettona who care for pottery might make a quick detour to the big village of Deruta some two miles south of the two towns. Glazed and painted jugs, plates, bowls, and tiles, displayed on roadside stands and in storefronts, greet the traveler passing Deruta on the Perugia-Todi highway. Walking up to the village center, on a steep hill, one sees several pottery factories and gaudily painted houses with elaborate majolica ornamentation. The town hall includes a picture gallery with works by local artists, and a ceramics museum. Deruta has been a center of the majolica industry since the Middle Ages, and at the height of its fortunes in the sixteenth century counted some fifty pottery workshops. A cooperative has recently revived the traditional Deruta ceramics industry.

✌ *The Young Tiber* ☙

Once in Perugia, no one will want to omit the half-hour trip to Assisi (p. 139ff.). The regional capital is also the obvious base for an excursion to Gubbio (p. 162ff.), and for exploring northern Umbria. The latter district is easily accessible by the E-45 super-highway and the Ferrovia Centrale Umbra (FCU), or Central Umbrian Railway. The blue trains of this nonstate railroad leisure-ly link Perugia's Sant'Anna and Ponte San Giovanni stations with Todi and Terni in the south and with Umbértide, Città di Castello and Sansepolcro (which already belongs to Tuscany) in the north.

The superhighway and the single-track private rail line run along the upper Tiber in a broad, green valley with friendly hills and mountains—the highest peaks around three thousand feet—on either side. The scenery is peaceful: grain, vegetable, and sun-flower fields in the valley; vineyards and olive plantations climb-ing the undramatic slopes; oak forests higher up. The towns and villages look well-off; low-slung factories turning out ceramics, furniture, building materials, and mechanical or electric compo-nents cluster near the population centers.

Umbértide (the stress is on the second syllable) on the east bank of the Tiber, twenty-two miles north of Perugia, has 14,000 residents. Until 1862 the town was known as Fratta Perugina or Fratta di Perugia; since there were more Frattas in the just-unified Kingdom of Italy, two years after the Umbrian Fratta had been incorporated into it the town fathers decided to change its official appellation. Wanting to pay homage to the new ruling dynasty, they found inspiration from the name of Crown Prince Umberto, who was then eighteen years old (he would become King of Italy as Umberto I in 1878 and be assassinated by an anarchist in 1900). Local scholars came up also with a similar-sounding historic reference: it seems that around A.D. 1000 one Uberto (without the *m*), a feudal lord of whom little is known, built himself a castle over Roman ruins on the spot that was to become Fratta and eventually Umbértide.

The fourteenth-century fortress that today distinguishes Umbértide may or may not be a direct successor to the stronghold of that half-forgotten Uberto. The mighty brick structure with its 120-foot-high battlemented square tower and three shorter round towers rises near a stream, the Reggia, that runs across the town to join the Tiber. Also near the stream is the freestanding, octagonal Church of Santa Maria della Reggia, containing a noteworthy fifteenth-century fresco of the Virgin Mary and Saints by an unidentified master. Another church in town, Santa Croce, is renowned for an altarpiece by Luca Signorelli (1516), depicting the Descent from the Cross. The painter was paid 86 florins for the dramatic composition, one of his masterpieces.

On a hill three miles east of Umbértide is the well-preserved, multiturreted Castle of Civitella Ranieri, which has been designated as a national landmark. It is named after its original lords, the Ranieri or Rainier family who claimed descent from a vassal of Charlemagne. In a garden stands the eighteenth-century statue of Ruggiero Ranieri, a famous condottiere who lived ninety years, from 1351 to 1441, and was commonly called Cane (dog) because of the shape he had chosen for his helmet.

Città di Castello, thirteen miles north of Umbértide, suggests by its name ("City of the Castle") the notion of a stronghold, and in Perugia and throughout northern Umbria is generally referred to simply as Castello. Its citizens however want to be called *tifernati* because in the times of the ancient Umbrians the town's name was Tifernum; the Romans later called it Tifernum Tiberinum to distinguish the town on the Tiber from other Tifernums in Italy. The Umbrian settlement apparently was a center of trade with the Etruscans on the opposite (west) bank of the Tiber, but remained self-governing until the Romans took over.

Today's visitor will find Città di Castello a very compact town with a population of 38,000, still in part enclosed by old walls, with narrow streets, a number of Renaissance palaces, a cathedral with an archaic cylindrical tower that is its main land-mark and symbol, and an outstanding collection of paintings. This Pinacoteca Comunale (Civic Picture Gallery) is indeed the region's most important art museum next to the National Gallery of Umbria in Perugia. It is housed in a splendidly restored wing of one of the several palaces that the conspicuous Vitelli family erected in the town, and a major reason for including Città di Castello in one's Umbrian itinerary.

Like other powerful Renaissance clans, and even more so than most, the upstart Vitellis had an urge for construction projects on a grand scale. The family was of plebeian origin, as everybody must have still remembered or known in the times of its greatness; its name prosaically means "calves." The Vitelli family had amassed great wealth through the wool trade, married into aristocracy, became confidants of some popes, and were by these rewarded for their services with noble titles and administrative jobs, and even-tually produced politicians, prelates, and condottieri.

There were setbacks, inevitable in those turbulent times. Vitellozzo II Vitelli, a famous and ruthless leader of mercenary soldiers, walked with other condottieri into a trap set by the even more faithless Cesare Borgia, the son of Pope Alexander VI, and on New Year's Eve of 1502 was strangled on orders from his captor. He was nevertheless granted the time to implore absolution from his sins by his murderer's father, the pontiff.

Before these vicissitudes, quite normal in the Renaissance age, the Vitellis governed Città di Castello and its territory throughout the second half of the fourteenth century and most of the fifteenth. Theoretically they acted as vicars, or lieutenants, of the papacy; actually they did very much what they liked, and raised funds for their own buildings.

The picture gallery is in the Palazzo Vitelli alla Cannoniera, erected in the sixteenth century on the site of a former gun foundry (whence its name). Its east front, looking out on a vast lawn, carries elegant gray-on-gray graffito decorations. The monumental staircase is richly frescoed with allegorical and heraldic pictures, the calf of the Vitelli coat of arms recurring in the imagery.

The paintings and other works of art in the twenty-one showrooms were mostly gathered from various churches. The prize exhibit is a religious banner that the young Raphael painted in 1500 or 1501; its two damaged sides are now separated, one showing St. Roch and St. Sebastian kneeling before the Trinity, the other carrying a Creation of Eve. It is the only work by Raphael that has remained in the town where he worked for some time after leaving Perugino's workshop in Perugia to paint independently. Opposite the church banner is a copy of the Sposalizio or Wedding of the Virgin (1504, cf p. 48). That famous Raphael painting was also executed in Città di Castello, but is now in Milan. Other works of Raphael's Città di Castello period are in various museums in Europe and in the United States.

In Room 12 is a Martyrdom of St. Sebastian by Luca Signorelli, painted 1497–98; every time I see it I am struck by the obvious glee with which Signorelli's torturers go about their fiendish work. The youthful Raphael was so impressed by that St. Sebastian that he made a design of it (now in Oxford). From his native Cortona, Signorelli repeatedly came to Città di Castello, and besides executing other works portrayed various members of the Vitelli family. The St. Sebastian is his only picture left in town; the rest of his sizable Città di Castello production is dispersed in the National Gallery of London and in diverse other collections.

Among the many other treasures of the Palazzo Vitelli alla Cannoniera is a Madonna and Child Enthroned with Six Angels by an unidentified fourteenth-century painter whom art historians call the Master of Città di Castello. Strong influences from the Sienese School have been pointed out in the impressive work. The other pictures in the gallery range from the second half of the thirteenth century to nineteenth-century neoclassicism. The restructured portico of the palazzo contains a few Roman antiquities and some sculptures including a graceful Assumption of the Virgin in terra-cotta from the Florence workshop of Andrea della Robbia (circa 1500).

Scattered about town are four other sumptuous former Vitelli mansions. The largest of them is the Palazzo Vitelli a Sant'Egidio, close to the eastern town walls, with fine ceiling frescoes by the Florentine sixteenth-century painter Cristofano Gherardi. It was built in 1540 by Giorgio Vasari, the architect and author of the fundamental *Lives of the Painters*, for the young Paolo Vitelli (who in

1571 would valorously fight the Turks in the Sea Battle of Lepanto). Across a vast garden is a lavishly decorated summer-house, the Palazzina Vitelli, with a charming loggia. Two other former Vitelli residences in the city serve mundane purposes today.

Also noteworthy is the elegant Palazzo Albizzini, left of Vasari's building. It now contains a collection of works by Alberto Burri (1915–95) that he donated to his native city, including some of his signature sackcloth creations. Other Burri pictures are on display in the former tobacco sheds on the southern outskirts.

The Cathedral of Città di Castello goes back to the eleventh century, but little of the original structure has survived. The cylindrical campanile with a rough, gray exterior and a brown, conical roof seems inspired by the early-medieval steeples of Ravenna. The cathedral was thoroughly rebuilt between the fourteenth and seventeenth centuries.

The cathedral museum holds a collection of sixth-century liturgical silver vessels that were found in a pilgrimage church on a hillside west of the Tiber in 1936, as well as the so-called *paliotto*. This is an embossed panel of gilt silver from the twelfth century with relief representations of Gospel episodes and saints; Pope Celestine II (1143–44), who was known as Guido di Castello before his elevation to the pontifical throne, gave the work to his hometown, it is assumed.

The City Hall (Palazzo Comunale), a Gothic building from the fourteenth century with rusticated walls and Gothic double windows, adjoins the cathedral. At a short distance is the Church of St. Francis (San Francesco), dating from the thirteenth century, but altered later. Inside is the so-called Vitelli Chapel, built by

Vasari for the dominant family; he also painted a Coronation of the Virgin and Saints on a wall (1564). Over an altar of the church is a copy of Raphael's Sposalizio, indicating the spot where the original (p. 68) once hung. A tablet near the church portal notes that Raphael painted some of his first works in town. The square on which the church stands is called Piazza Raffaello Sanzio; the town's leading hotel, the four-star Tiferno, faces it. The stands of a lively outdoor market line the nearby Via del Popolo.

Two miles east of Città di Castello is a little sulphur-spring spa, Terme di Fontecchio, mentioned already by Pliny the Younger (A.D. 61–113). The Tiber, skirting the southwest corner of Città di Castello, near the picture gallery, after about forty miles from its source at an altitude of 4,160 feet on Mount Fiumaiolo in the Tuscan-Emilian Apennines, looks most of the time like a placid stream rather than a river. After persistent rains, however, it will become a roaring torrent (p. x).

Every March boating enthusiasts from Italy and other countries gather in Città di Castello for the International Tiber Canoeing Event. It is not a race. Participants cover 180 of the river's 251 miles in ten days, unhurriedly paddling along, enjoying the sights of Umbria and Latium, and spending the nights in tents ashore. Buses with provisions, luggage, and camp followers accompany the canoe fleet on roads along the banks. The Tiber voyage ends in Rome's north near the Milvian Bridge, the sturdy stone structure that the ancients built for chariots and marching legions, and which is still being used by pedestrians, after motor vehicles were banned from it after World War II.

The Tiber flows into Umbria from Tuscany eight miles north of Città di Castello; Tuscan influences, not surprisingly, are strong in the city's dialect, customs, cooking, architecture, and art. The Vitelli clan and many other *tifernati* always maintained close ties with Tuscany and that region's illustrious capital, Florence.

From Città di Castello it is only ten miles to Sansepolcro, the birthplace of Piero della Francesca, which is in Tuscany. Two miles closer is the administrative border between that region and Umbria. For hundreds of years it was a veritable frontier with guards, soldiers, and customs inspectors on either side; in the south were the States of the Church, in the north was Tuscany—subsequently a republic, a duchy, and a grand duchy.

That border, oddly, wasn't precisely demarcated in the Tiber area, allegedly because officials from the Vatican and Florence had fixed it one-sidedly without bothering to consult with one another. A consequence was that the small village of Cospaia on a hill east of the river (now reachable by a road branching off Superhighway E-45) became a no-man's-land. From 1440 to 1826 the village was practically a tiny republic, run by the parish priest (who had no bishop above him) jointly with local elders. Inevitably Cospaia turned into a smugglers' paradise and a haven for fugitives from papal or Tuscan law.

At long last Pope Leo XII and Grand Duke Leopold II of Tuscany agreed that the nuisance had to end, and that the dwarf republic should be split between their respective domains. The States of the Church got fifty-five households with 293 residents, Tuscany ten households with 80 people (families were numerous then). To sweeten the deal for the villagers, all Cospaia girls who were to wed in 1826 were promised dowries by the new authorities, which is said to have caused a record crop of births in 1827.

More consequential was another privilege accorded the now-papal part of Cospaia: Its inhabitants were authorized to grow tobacco. The culture of the plant, then still considered exotic and the source of a dangerous vice, had until 1826 been banned in the States of the Church. Tobacco was being grown clandestinely nevertheless while Cospaia had been a center of highly lucrative tobacco contraband. From the now-legal tobacco fields close to the Tuscan border the culture quickly spread down the Tiber valley and into other low-lying parts of Umbria. A tobacco-curing plant was built near Città di Castello. The villagers of Cospaia, after 1826 obliged to pay taxes to the pontifical state or to Tuscany—and later to the unified Italian Kingdom—may have long looked with nostalgia at the motto that their independent forebears had engraved on the architrave of their parish church: PERPETUA ET FIRMA LIBERTAS (perpetual and strong freedom—especially freedom from taxation).

3

⤞⁖⤝

The Road to Assisi I

Ask any educated Italian who was the greatest Umbrian in all history, and the answer will be "St. Francis of Assisi." Mystics and ascetics revere him as a paragon of perfection; greens and pacifists praise him as a nature lover and an advocate of nonviolence; avowed atheists take part in the periodic peace marches from Perugia to Assisi, honoring the saint together with believers.

To the Roman Catholic Church and other Christian denominations the founder of the Franciscan order is a champion of evangelical poverty and humility; Pope Pius XII in 1939 proclaimed him patron saint of Italy. As far as Umbria is concerned, St. Francis may also be regarded as the heavenly promoter of the tourist business. In a palazzo near the Basilica of St. Francis in Assisi, the State University of Perugia maintains a special department that trains travel agents and grants master degrees in the science of tourism.

The birthplace of St. Francis draws pilgrims and sightseers year-round from all over the world; major events in Rome or Florence—each about 115 miles distant from Assisi—will swell the stream of visitors. Travelers journeying to Assisi from either city should avoid rushing the trip but stop on the way in more than one place to savor the region's uniqueness.

Leaving Rome northward by car or railroad, one is at the traffic hub of Orte in less than an hour; the town is the gate to Umbria. Orte, near the confluence of the Tiber and Nera rivers fifty miles north of Rome, with a population of nearly 10,000 and a cramped, old town nucleus on a hill, isn't, frankly, much to look at. Its modern section in the plain with its rail station, marshaling yards, access roads, service stations, and flimsy architecture is utilitarian. Umbria starts almost immediately the moment your train, bus, or car turns northeast. The Nera valley and the hills will soon seem greener than did the landscape—northern Latium—you just left.

First, however, the rail tracks and the highway traverse a plain with an electric power plant and sprawling chemical works. Despite recent pollution-control measures, the air is foul and the Nera River looks muddy with industrial effluents. On a nearby hill stands the medieval Montero Castle, built over the ruins of an ancient Roman villa.

Then comes the real entrance to Umbria, a dramatic gorge cut by the Nera in the geological epoch when the river forced its way across a chain of the Apennines. The foaming water flows in many bends between steep rocks and forests of olive trees, willows, poplars, and evergreen oaks.

If you travel by train, look out of the car's right side at the northern exit from the ravine. You will see the impressive remains of an ancient engineering feat, the Bridge of Augustus. It spanned the Nera with four daring arches; the one at the east bank, sixty-two feet high, still stands, while only the piers of the other three remain. Wooden or stone bridges at this spot are known to have existed even before the Via Flaminia (p. xx) was built in the third century B.C. Emperor Augustus had an earlier bridge here greatly strengthened, creating what was one of the most imposing and elegant river crossings in the Roman Empire's heartlands.

After centuries of service the 525-foot-long bridge collapsed either in an earthquake or owing to a lack of maintenance or as a result of military action during the barbarian invasions. The Via Flaminia was diverted eastward. A new stone bridge a few yards south of the ruined ancient one was built in the Middle Ages, and was repeatedly renovated. It was damaged by bombs toward the end of World War II, and was repaired in the immediate postwar period.

⌒ Cyclopean Walls ∾

Before proceeding to Narni, Terni, and Spoleto the visitor might profitably take the turnoff northward on National Route No. 205, near the ruined Roman bridge and the new one, to see one of Umbria's oldest towns, Amelia. The seven-and-a-half-mile side trip reveals bucolic scenery—vineyards, clumps of oaks and rows of olive trees on soft-shaped hills, grazing sheep, friendly hamlets.

The highway rises, and twenty-five-foot-high walls come into sight. Their basis are huge, irregular rocks, neatly fitted together without mortar. They support regularly hewn stone blocks that experts have easily determined to be Etruscan work first, and ancient Roman reinforcements higher up. The fortifications, ten feet broad in some stretches, were again strengthened in the Middle Ages. So far, so good—even the layman will recognize the various later phases of wall construction. But what about those jagged foundations?

Defenses formed by masses of big stones heaped one above the other have long been called "cyclopean," as if mythical titans had built them. One wonders, in fact, about the technology, tools, and manpower used in quarrying, transporting, adapting, and piling up those enormous rocks. Today grass and other vegetation grow out of some of the cracks in the walls, but there isn't much space for their roots, so well are the rugged stone faces put together. So-called cyclopean walls can be seen in various parts of Italy, but those of Amelia are among the best-preserved.

They are supposed to be the work of a Bronze Age tribe that inhabited the region before the Umbrians arrived from the north; in their turn the latter were, here as elsewhere, eventually dominated by the Etruscans before the Romans subdued them all. The builders of the "cyclopean" walls that can be seen in Amelia and in some other Umbrian towns are often called Pelasgians, but there is nothing to back up that attribution. Prehistorians conceive the Pelasgians as an Aegean people speaking a non-Greek language; Homer mentions them as allies of the Trojans. Pelasgians were reported in Crete and mainland Greece in antiquity, and some of them may have crossed the Adriatic Sea, drifted into the interior of the Italian peninsula, and settled in such places as Amelia. But all this is mere conjecture.

The fact is, the Etruscans and the Romans who strengthened the original fortifications that encircle the hill town knew that Amelia even then was very old. Cato the Elder, who pondered about the origins of Italian cities, put the time of Amelia's foundation at a date that would correspond to 1134 B.C.

At one time during the Middle Ages when large chunks of central Italy were in the hands of barbarians, Amelia saw a lot of military and civilian traffic. The Via Flaminia (now National Route No. 3) between Rome and the Adriatic was controlled over long stretches by the fierce Lombards and was therefore shunned by many transports and travelers. An alternate route bypassing the Teutonic-held areas went from Orte by way of Amelia, Perugia, and Gubbio to the Adriatic coast and was called Via Amerina (Amelia was Ameria in Latin).

For many centuries after that early-medieval epoch until today Amelia remained outside the major routes of communication. The railroad age bypassed it (but Narni's distant rail station is officially called "Narni-Amelia"). Mass tourism has left Amelia alone too. Some Roman families today own weekend homes in the town, yet it has remained blissfully quiet, still living to a great extent off the good farmland all around. The figs of Amelia are nationally famous. An exhibition of agricultural machines is held in Amelia every September.

The little town is well off. While visitors must park their cars outside the walls, there is plenty of motor traffic in the narrow, sloping streets inside; two-car families are no rarity here. Like many other Umbrian towns, Amelia has a left-wing administration; the longtime leader of the Communist-controlled National Labor Confederation, Luciano Lama, who was a widely respected moderate, served for many years as its mayor, resigning only shortly before his death in 1996.

The main entrance into the town is through the so-called Roman Gate, a Baroque doorway surrounded by embrasures, built in 1703. Left and right are lengths of the Cyclopean-Etruscan-Roman-medieval walls. The rising Via della Repubblica, the central street, would seem unchanged for centuries—if there weren't a new fashion boutique halfway up. The thirteenth-century Church of San Francesco on a little square has a facade in pink stone with a magnificent double rose window as its sole ornament; adjacent is a peaceful cloister.

The domed cathedral, visible for many miles, crowns the hill. Its twelve-sided, flat-topped bell tower was erected in 1050 with fragments saved from earlier constructions and coarse stones that now look livid and weather-wasted. The church went up at the same time as the campanile, but it was completely rebuilt in the seventeenth century and lacks architectural distinction. The lofty platform on which the cathedral and its tower rise commands vistas of the uncluttered countryside all around and of a deep ravine north and west of Amelia through which a little stream flows toward the Tiber. Returning to the main lines of communication between Rome and the heart of Umbria, the traveler enjoys fine views of the houses and towers of Narni on its cliffs.

From the Orte-Terni roads (National Route No. 204 and Superhighway E-45), a highway climbs from a turnoff near the Narni-Amelia railroad to the ancient town of Narni on its 400-foot-high rock. The Umbrians had a sizable settlement there, known as Nequinum. When the Romans conquered the lofty place, they called it Narnia after the river Nar (now Nera) flowing at its feet toward the Tiber.

ᴖ Cliffs and Workshops ᴖ

Narni today is a breezy town of medieval towers, dilapidated buildings on narrow streets or at the edge of nearly perpendicular cliffs, and quite a few new constructions. A massive, somber castle on a separate hill that had until recently been used as a penitentiary was, during my latest visit, being restructured to serve as a cultural center. It was one of many strongholds that Cardinal Albornoz (p. 21) had built in the fourteenth century.

Narni's cathedral, in Romanesque style, is from the twelfth century, with a graceful Renaissance portico. Other noteworthy architecture includes the Loggia dei Priori, a porch with two high arches, once erected to adorn the seat of the town government; a tower from the fourteenth century facing an elongated square; and the medieval town hall. The former Church of San Domenico, from the thirteenth century, is now a museum with Roman antiquities and a small picture gallery containing an Annunciation by Benozzo Gozzoli as well as works by minor Umbrian masters.

Toward northeast Narni looks down on the valley of the Nera, wide open here, at the city of Terni at a distance of ten miles, and at Apennine chains in a bluish haze behind it. Below Narni's rock spreads an industrial zone with many medium-size and small enterprises and workshops as well as a modern residential section near the Narni-Amelia railroad station (now frequently called Narni Scalo). The Nera in the river's final reaches is indigo-colored from chemical wastes. Lower Narni almost joins the sprawl of Terni in an eight-mile industrial corridor, although truck farms too keep thriving in the well-watered plain.

Approaching Terni on the superhighway or by train, the traveler is greeted, on the left, by a new high-rise building that is a miniskyscraper; it is a fitting introduction to Umbria's powerhouse. The abundant waters of the Nera and its tributary, the Serra, turned mills already in antiquity. Today the energy potential of the two merging rivers is thoroughly exploited by several power plants.

Italy chose Terni toward the end of the nineteenth century as the site for a big armaments works that eventually covered the full cycle from steelmaking to turning out big guns and millions of the famed Model 91 rifle that generations of army recruits learned to fire. Mechanical, chemical, and textile industries also installed themselves in the Terni area, which by 1910 had become the "Italian Manchester," employing several thousand workers. During World War I the demand for weapons led to further expansion of Terni's steelmaking capacity and armaments output.

Mussolini's dictatorship promoted also the production of synthetic rubber in Terni in its efforts to lessen the country's dependance on imports of strategic materials. At the beginning of World War II the Terni steel, arms, and rubber plants were working day and night, but soon Allied air attacks began taking them out. In 108 heavy raids, Terni's industrial sections and much of other neighborhoods were bombed into rubble.

Terni and its industrial park east of its core were rebuilt after the war's end; the government-owned steelworks was again among Italy's biggest. The nation, however, soon discovered that it was producing more steel than it could use or sell abroad; as happened in other European steel centers, the rigors of privatization, restructuring, downsizing, and reconversion also gripped Terni. Many of its workers were put on short hours or laid off. Today the Terni furnaces turn out special steels, and are controlled by Krupp of Germany. Instead of trying to make and market synthetic rubber, as under Mussolini, Terni now produces plastics. New mechanical, electronic, and soft-goods enterprises have sprung up.

The city, however, clings to its old metallic image. In 1995 Terni erected a one hundred-foot-high steel obelisk, designed by the sculptor Arnaldo Pomodoro, on a main street near its center, the Corso del Popolo. Local steelworkers toiled for 13,000 man-hours to fashion the new landmark, which weighs forty metric tons and is topped by a glittering spur, visible from many points in the city and its surroundings.

Rebuilt after the devastations of World War II, Terni is now largely modern; most streets are straight and intersect at right angles. Five city blocks from the new railroad station is Piazza Tacito where the prefecture building, in a postwar neo-Baroque style with a pretentious loggia on top, is facing a new, circular fountain. The name of the square in a modern neighborhood that was one of the main targets of World War II bombers is very old: Terni insists on having been the birthplace of the historian Cornelius Tacitus (circa A.D. 55–circa 120). The claim rests on nothing more than the fact that a wealthy Roman official, Marcus Claudius Tacitus, who was emperor for only five months (275–76), was a native of what is today Terni and then was known by its old Umbrian name, Interamna ("between the rivers," meaning the Nera and the Serra). He would assert descent from the author of the *Annals* and other famed works.

Stone Age finds are evidence that at the river confluence Terni was inhabited since prehistoric times. In antiquity it was an important trade center; the ruined amphitheater near the Civic Gardens on the southwestern outskirts could accommodate 10,000 spectators. The nearby cathedral dates from the thirteenth century, but was rebuilt in the seventeenth century. The edifice suffered only minor damages during the air raids—in fact, they improved it: The impact of the bomb blasts bared a Romanesque rose window in the interior that had been long forgotten.

The bombs of World War II did demolish the clock tower of the old City Hall on Piazza del Popolo, Terni's central square. Now a steel-and-glass superstructure rather incongruously crowns the restored building. From the City Hall to the Piazza Tacito runs the city's major shopping street, Via Cornelio Tacito.

The prefecture on Piazza Tacito supervises the province of Terni, the smaller of Umbria's two administrative subdivisions, which includes such centers as Orvieto, Narni, and Amelia. There is talk every now and then of creating a third Umbrian province with headquarters in either Spoleto or Foligno, and assigning to it some territory now belonging to Perugia province. The prospect of such bureaucratic changes adds to the intense rivalry between Umbrian cities and towns; I have heard many Perugians and Spoletans speak with undisguised disdain of Terni, a sentiment amply reciprocated by the Ternani.

The summary description of Terni I have provided above will hardly induce the reader to set any length of time aside for a visit to Umbria's second city. I myself usually stop in Terni on my way to or from other Umbrian destinations or the Adriatic coast only long enough for a cappuccino and one of the renowned local *cornetti* (croissants). Many rail travelers change trains in Terni, which is a hub of branch lines to Todi and the upper Tiber valley as well as to Rieti, Aquila, and Suloma in the Abruzzo region, but few of them bother to stroll into the city even though they would have time for doing so, preferring to wait for their connection at the station. Most hotel guests in Terni aren't tourists but business people or citizens with matters pending at the prefecture or the law courts.

◡: Lovers' Saint :◡

Yet there is one category of visitors who come to the steel city for an eminently romantic reason: St. Valentine is not only the patron saint of Terni but also the celestial advocate of lovers anywhere in the world. His remains with a bishop's miter on his skull and a crosier beside the skeleton can be seen behind glass under the altar in the choir of the basilica and parish church dedicated to him.

It is not easy to find the sanctuary of lovers in an unlovely suburb on Terni's south. Motorists arriving on the superhighway from Orte see yellow signs with the outline of the church and SAN VALENTINO on it that guide them as far as a bridge across the Nera River; but then, when a driver would need them most, there are no more signs and one has to ask for directions. (If men do the driving, women usually do the asking.) Eventually, at the end of a short, rising street in a scruffy neighborhood, the church becomes visible.

It is a beige building in undistinguished Baroque style such as one can see in hundreds of villages up and down Italy. It was erected in 1618, replacing an ancient church on the spot where St. Valentine is believed to have been buried. Ancient Christian tradition has it that he was a native of Interamna (Terni) and was educated in Rome. Coming back home as a deacon, Valentinus was consecrated bishop of Interamna by the bishop of Foligno, St. Felicianus, in A.D. 197 or 203. He was martyred by beheading under Emperor Aurelian in 273 and was later proclaimed the patron saint of his native city.

St. Valentine's reputation as a supporter of lovers is founded on legends of miracles he achieved for young couples, and about his reputed custom of presenting newlyweds with a red rose as a symbol of lasting commitment. One story narrates that the saint astounded his flock around A.D. 245 by permitting a Christian girl, Serapia, to wed Sabinus, a Roman knight who was a pagan. The knight soon became himself a Christian; when his young wife died he prayed for the grace of being permitted to join her in heaven, and expired shortly thereafter.

The presumed body of St. Valentine, located in a lead coffin, was exhumed in 1605. It was kept in Terni's cathedral until the basilica dedicated to him was completed. In a macabre twist, the saint's skull was believed to have somehow ended up in Austria, where it was treasured in a reliquary by the Habsburg dynasty for three centuries. In 1625 Archduke Leopold of Austria returned the skull to Terni, but kept one of the saint's teeth as a token relic.

The basilica, in charge of Carmelite monks, draws visitors all year long, and especially on February 14, St. Valentine's Day. Many couples want to get married then and there; others come to renew their marriage vows. Father Orlando Pietrobono, who for the last ten years has been prior of the basilica, says: "They come from all over the world to Terni, to the church of the sainted patron of people in love; many bring red roses, some implore the saint to help them regain lost love, or pray for recovery from illness from which they or their spouse suffer." The prior reports that among the love pilgrims the Japanese are particularly numerous. "They hold in their hands scraps of paper on which they have written about their emotional problems, and before leaving ask me to burn those paper messages in front of St. Valentine's altar. Thus, they say, they may hope that their wishes will be granted— a belief derived from their Shintoist traditions." It seems the prior obliges the Japanese.

Apart from what Terni means to devotees of St. Valentine, the city may not have much to offer to sightseers, but it provides access to one of the lesser-known beauty spots of Umbria, the Lake of Piediluco. Rail travelers change at Terni station into the diesel train plying the branch line to Rieti in the Sabine district, and get out at the Marmore stop. Nearby are impressive waterfalls (Cascate delle Marmore), which the ancient Romans created in a bold drainage project in the third century B.C. The name Marmore refers to the marble plates with which the ancient engineers lined parts of the cascades.

It was a general and consul, Manius Curius Dentatus, who, in 272 B.C., built a canal to stave off the recurrent flooding of a basin around what is today the city of Rieti by opening an outlet of the Velino River into the Nera. His canal, widened in the sixteenth century, is still in use. The water of the Velino precipitates into the Nera in three large leaps of 65, 330, and 195 feet four and a half miles east of Terni. By road, one reaches the falls from Terni on National Route No. 79. Today the cascades are much less to look at than when Byron marveled at them and in *Childe Harold* (IV, 72) called them "horribly beautiful." Most of the water is now being diverted, especially on weekdays, to a big power plant and for other industrial uses.

From the waterfalls it is about two miles on National Route

No. 79 to the town of Piediluco at 1,200 feet above sea level in a setting of wooded hills. The irregularly shaped blue lake is a sight of great peacefulness; the trouble is that at present it is very polluted by raw sewage.

⌣: *Festival City* :~

A new superhighway from Orte (National Route No. 204) leaps across Terni's northern outskirts and industrial area on high piers, permitting motor travelers to bypass the busy city altogether, and many do just that. Less than twenty miles to the north is Spoleto, and that's quite a different story. That city, now again vital and well off, is one of Umbria's most remarkable places, an outdoor museum and artistic treasure trove.

When Gian Carlo Menotti during the late 1950s conceived the plan to organize a new festival as a periodic event to present old and modern music and other arts from Europe and America, he cast around for an appropriate site near Rome. Among other places, the ancient town of Viterbo, sixty-five miles northwest of the Italian capital, caught his attention. It would have been a good choice, but the local authorities appeared lukewarm toward the Italian-American composer's idea. Eventually he selected Spoleto, which was more forthcoming.

Just when Menotti first visited Spoleto and soon decided to realize his festival plans there, the city was going through a socioeconomic crisis. The old soft-coal pits in its vicinity, long unprofitable, had at last been abandoned, and several hundred miners were jobless. Spoleto had a sole third-class hotel, a few even simpler inns, and only modest eating places. Most guests at the 1958 debut of the Festival of Two Worlds returned to Rome after the end of the performances, arriving in the capital long after midnight.

Today Spoleto is much fancier. The city has five first-class hotels, a score of other commendable ones, and well over fifty restaurants and cafés. Pubs, night spots, designer-label boutiques, and jewelry shops have sprouted all over town. To deepen the old, genuine quaintness of the place, the municipal administration had new lanterns that imitate old-fashioned ones installed in central neighborhoods; their soft light, however, doesn't help much if you're looking for a street sign at night.

The Festival of Two Worlds has made Spoleto's name familiar to people abroad who otherwise would ignore it. Since 1977 there has been a Spoleto U.S.A. event in Charleston, South Carolina; after bitter battles over control, Menotti washed his hands of it in 1993. Menotti's original festival in Spoleto too has tended to assume a life of its own—independent of its founder—since the early 1990s. City Hall wanted a bigger say in the event's management, and opposed Menotti's plan to entrust its future guidance to his adoptive son Francis.

The festival at any rate has brought plenty of cosmopolitan visitors and new businesses to the city. Big-name conductors, stage directors, and singers contributed to the opera productions; Margot Fonteyn, Rudolph Nureyev, and Mikhail Baryshnikov danced in Spoleto; Alexander Calder (1898–1978) designed sets for Mozart's *Don Giovanni* and sculpted what was to become a local landmark, his Teodolapio (p. 94).

Some foreigners bought houses in Spoleto. One of them was Gustav Mahler's only surviving daughter, Anna, who was a sculptor. She lived in the city a few months every year, and shortly before her death in 1988 told me she didn't care for the festival crowd. I too preferred the city at other times, I said to her, outside the few weeks in June and early July when Spoleto has its brief, heady season of musical and theatrical performances with an international flavor and a good deal of un-Umbrian snobbery.

Before starting any systematic sightseeing in the singularly picturesque city, it's a good idea to stroll at random around the old neighborhoods with their gray, sloping streets, their many stairways under little arches, their severe Romanesque and Gothic churches, and their medieval palaces, and get the feel of the place. One passageway in the lower part of town, claimed to be "Italy's narrowest street," hardly leaves space for two persons to pass each other; the official directory lists it as Vicolo Bacia Femmine ("Kiss the Women Lane").

If you wish to see a good cross-section of Spoleto's 38,000 residents, be at the hours of the daily *struscio*—late morning or afternoon—in the straight Corso Mazzini, halfway up the city, or in the Piazza della Libertà at that street's southern end. All around town there is much provincial charm to savor.

At some spots that are now semicentral, the remains of the oldest city walls are visible. They are "cyclopean" defenses like those of Amelia (p. 78). After the Pelasgians or whatever other Bronze Age people piled up these massive irregular rocks, the Umbrians, Romans, medieval Germanic tribes, and papal governors who successively held sway in Spoleto kept building fortifications. Stretches of city walls from various epochs can be discerned in several parts of the city.

The number and nature of Roman ruins prove that Spoleto was important almost from 241 B.C., when it became a colony of Rome. In 217 B.C. the city repelled an attack by Hannibal, who had just annihilated a Roman army at Lake Trasimeno. A medieval town gate in Spoleto's south, on the spot where a much older structure once stood, is called Porta Fuga, or Flight Gate—an allusion to the story that the Carthaginians were turned back here.

Siege craft doesn't seem to have been the forte of Hannibal, although before his invasion of Italy he beleaguered and conquered the Roman town of Saguntum in Spain with apparent ease. Instead of trying to take Spoleto and proceeding to Rome, the Cathaginian general turned northeast to march toward the Adriatic Sea and southern Italy. He apparently fooled the hastily formed legions that Rome had sent after him by a stratagem: He had torches tied to the horns of 2,000 oxen, and drove them at night through an easy pass near what is today the town of Gualdo Tadino (p. 174) while his troops stealthily crossed another mountain pass. The feint, Hannibal's "ox trick," succeeded, and his forces remained strong enough to inflict on the Romans another terrible defeat at Cannae.

In Spoleto an old story is told of the city's defenders having poured boiling oil on Hannibal's troops from the walls, forcing them to withdraw. The high, square Oil Tower near the Flight Gate is supposed to owe its name to the episode. However, that tower is from the thirteenth century, its lower part being encased in an even younger building. Another version of the old boiling-oil anecdote would have had it poured on the soldiers of Emperor Frederick Barbarossa who in 1155 sacked the town, but the Oil Tower had not yet been built even then. The slender tower possibly played a role in some other medieval siege in which the city's defenders resorted to the time-honored stratagem of dousing assailants with seering liquid; Spoleto was since the oldest times abundantly supplied with oil from the olive groves all around.

In the second century B.C. the Romans built an amphitheater

in what are now Spoleto's northeastern outskirts; measuring 390 feet by 295 feet, it was then one of the largest constructions of its kind in their domains. In the sixth century A.D. the Ostrogoths of King Totila transformed the complex into a fortress; eight centuries later Cardinal Albornoz had it demolished and had much of its stone blocks used for the construction of the hilltop fortress that looms above Spoleto. Some arches and other remains of the Roman amphitheater are still visible in the courtyards of the army barracks on the Via dell'Anfiteatro.

The Roman Theater, a different structure off one of the city's liveliest squares, Piazza della Libertà, has instead been freed of the superstructures that hid its ruins until after World War II. It serves now for outdoor shows and concerts during the Festival of Two Worlds. The shell-shaped spectators' space, descending in sixteen stone steps to the orchestra pit and stage, seats several hundred people.

Other noteworthy Roman ruins are a triumphal arch, a bridge, and a dwelling. The arch, formed of travertine blocks, was erected in A.D. 23 in honor of Drusus, son of Emperor Tiberius, and of Germanicus, the emperor's adoptive son, to provide a solemn entrance to what was then the forum, the center of the city's public and commercial life. Originally thirty feet high, the monument, now squeezed between the much younger houses of the Via dell'Arco di Druso, seems short because in nearly two millennia the street surface has risen by five feet. The former forum is, as Piazza del Mercato, still a locality of commerce; a weekly outdoor market is held in it.

The remains of an eighty-foot-long bridge from the first century B.C., which spanned the Tessino stream, can be seen near the Piazza Garibaldi in the town's northern corner. To the Spoletans the structure is the "sanguinary" bridge (Ponte Sanguinario), linked to the belief that early Christian martyrs shed their blood in the nearby amphitheater.

Amid the vaulted foundations of City Hall and under the square in front of it, parts of a comfortable Roman private home with an atrium, various chambers, a bath, mosaic floors, and traces of frescoes can be visited. One theory is that the house belonged to Vespasia Polla, mother of the first-century-A.D. Emperor Vespasian. Sightseers descend to the Roman dwelling from a small door around the corner, left of the City Hall facade.

From the oblong Piazza del Municipio a broad stairway leads up to the entrance of the three-story City Hall, which is surmounted by a gray, square tower. The building houses a picture gallery in vast second-floor rooms that serve also as setting for civil weddings with the mayor or a deputy officiating.

The municipal art collection provides a chance for familiarizing oneself with the Spoletan painter Lo Spagna. This was the nickname of Giovanni di Pietro (circa 1450–1528) because he was supposedly of Spanish descent. Little is known of his early life, but around 1500 he became a citizen of Spoleto and married a local girl, Santina Capoferri; their daughter wed his Sicilian pupil, Iacopo Siculo. Lo Spagna himself had started out as an assistant of Perugino and later became strongly influenced by Raphael, so much so that some works by the Spoletan were for some time attributed to the more famous painter from Urbino.

A prolific artist like Perugino, Lo Spagna painted many angelic-looking Madonnas and saints, and depicted the Umbrian landscape as backgrounds in many works; his often facile style seems to anticipate the florid mannerism of the late sixteenth century. The City Hall collection includes one of Lo Spagna's masterpieces, a Madonna and Child with Four Saints, as well as frescoes that he painted in Cardinal Albornoz's fortress, and which were later detached. The picture gallery contains also works by other Umbrian painters, several of them transferred from local edifices.

Spoleto's oldest churches go back to the early Middle Ages, but the Teutonic rulers who from A.D. 569 dominated the city and a vast territory around it for nearly six hundred years left no monument. The chronicles, nevertheless, record the power of the dukedom, which was governed first by Lombard and then by Frankish princes. Spoleto remembers with pride its medieval role as the capital of a quasi-independent feudal state; there is a Street of the Dukes near Market Square, and one of the leading hotels is the Albergo dei Duchi. Although the initial impact of the invading, long-bearded barbarians must have been jarring enough for the Umbrian-Roman inhabitants of ancient Spoleto, the ruling Germanic upper class and the local population seem to have adjusted to each other over the centuries. The sparsely documented history of the high Middle Ages is explored by a specialized institute, which has its seat in the seventeenth-century Palazzo degli Ancaiani, and periodically organizes international scholarly symposia in the city.

A curious artistic reminder of Lombard domination in Spoleto was created by the American sculptor Alexander Calder. Visitors arriving in the city by train cannot miss it the moment they step out of the post–World War II railroad station. It is one of Calder's steel stabiles, fifty-nine feet high and forty-six feet large, suggesting a stylized, long-necked prehistoric animal. The contrast between the black, abstract sculpture and the ochre-colored, low station building is striking. Calder's towering work was assembled in 1962 as part of an international open-air exhibition that filled Spoleto's streets and squares with modern sculptures; most of them left the city after the show, but Calder's stabile and a few other steel artifacts have remained. The Spoletans call the Calder work simply "The Horse," although its official title is Teodolapio.

In a random poll, I recently asked ten local people what that name meant; no one knew. Teodolapio is the Italian form of the name of Spoleto's third Lombard duke (A.D. 601–653), one of two sons of the dynasty's founder, Faroald I (circa A.D. 570–591). Theodolapius succeeded in transforming Spoleto and much land around it into a principality that was virtually independent of the Lombard kings in Pavia, far to the north, during a stormy period when even a Lombard military grab for Rome seemed a possibility. It fell to an artist from the New World to shape a monument of the early-medieval ruler with steel from the furnaces of nearby Terni.

The Lombard lords of Spoleto presumably worshiped in a church that stood at the spot where the present cathedral rises. It was replaced around A.D. 1000 by an edifice in Romanesque style, which was heavily damaged when Barbarossa conquered and nearly destroyed Spoleto. The cathedral was restored, and Pope Innocent III, one of the most forceful ecclesiastical figures of the Middle Ages, reconsecrated it in 1198. Architects and artists continued working on the church for centuries. The edifice in a hollow near the eastern corner of the city, with Albornoz's fortress glowering from the hill above it, is the primary monument of Spoleto and one of the most beautiful cathedrals in Italy.

Walking down the low steps from the square in front of City Hall (Piazza del Municipio) to the broader Cathedral Square (Piazza del Duomo), I am impressed every time by the church's singular facade and the mighty square tower at its left. It is a Romanesque-Byzantine-Gothic-Renaissance assemblage that comes off spectacularly well. There are no fewer than eight Gothic rose windows of different sizes in that facade, not just one as in the front of Orvieto's cathedral. Below the three upper ones is a mosaic of a blessing Jesus between the Virgin Mary and St. John on gold ground, dated A.D. 1207 and clearly inspired by Byzantine art. The superbly sculptured Romanesque portal is under a porch with five classical arches, an addition from the end of the fifteenth century. The lower part of the campanile was erected in the twelfth century with travertine blocks taken from the ruined amphitheater; the tower's bell loft, in pinkish stones, and its pointed top are from the fifteenth and sixteenth centuries.

After the elegance of the facade the cathedral's interior is, to my taste, a letdown with its cool Baroque formalism, the result of remodeling in the seventeenth century. Only patches of the pavement are from the original Romanesque church. The artwork on the walls is more remarkable. In a chapel immediately at the right of the entrance are fragments of frescoes by Pinturicchio. The apse contains the last works by the Florentine master Fra Filippo Lippi (1406–1469), the disciple of Fra Angelico and teacher of Botticelli. His frescoes represent the Annunciation, Birth of Jesus, Death of Mary, and, in the semidome, a brilliant Coronation of Mary.

The group at the right side of the Death of Mary episode is said to include a self-portrait of Fra Filippo and the likeness of his son Filippino (a product of the love affair between the gifted Carmelite friar and his Florentine model Lucrezia Buti) as well as of his pupil Fra Diamante who completed the frescoes after Fra Filippo's sudden death. There were rumors in Spoleto at the time that the ardent friar had been poisoned in some romantic intrigue. The tomb of Fra Filippo is in the right transept; it was commissioned by Lorenzo the Magnificent, the painter-friar's patron in Medicean Florence, and designed by the latter's son Filippino. The celebrated humanist Politian composed the Latin epitaph, which praises Fra Filippo as a person and artist.

Cathedral Square becomes a vast sounding board at outdoor concerts during the Festival of Two Worlds. The orchestra plays in front of the church's portico, and listeners fill the piazza and the stairs leading to it. The wall of rough stone blocks on the southeastern side of Cathedral Square contains the tomb of the American conductor Thomas Schippers (1930–1977), who was a close associate of Menotti and his Spoleto project. As the first musical director of the Festival of Two Worlds, Schippers conducted Verdi's *Macbeth*, produced by Luchino Visconti, at its inauguration on June 5, 1958. Near the laconic tablet marking the tomb are a fountain and a Roman sarcophagus. Menotti's palazzo too is on the square's southeast side.

The opposite side of Cathedral Square is in part taken up by the Teatro Caio Melisso, a graceful rococo theater from the eighteenth century; it had become a movie house before being restored for the festival. Chamber opera and other performances suited for its small stage are now produced here. The 400-seat theater is named after Caius Melissus, a Spoletan dramatist and freedman of Maecenas, the friend of Emperor Augustus.

Spoleto's other major stage, the 600-seat Teatro Nuovo on Piazza Beniamino Gigli in the lower part of the city, was built around the middle of the nineteenth century, and also offers festival performances. Its period curtain depicts what is, somewhat chauvinistically, described as "Hannibal's Defeat Below the Walls of Spoleto," with plenty of ancient helmets, horsemanship, and swordplay, but no boiling oil.

On the west side of the Teatro Caio Melisso, reachable over stairs descending left of the cathedral tower, is a park, Piazza della Signoria, over a cliff commanding a fine view of the lower city and the plain in the northwest. A sign warns that dog walkers are liable to fines from the equivalent of about $3 to an incredible $625. In other words, dogs are banned from the airy square. The severe, unfinished Palazzo della Signoria ("Palace of the Lords") on the park's south side was built in the fourteenth century for the city's aristocratic rulers on the ruins of what is believed to have been the official residence of the Lombard and Frankish dukes. The unfinished construction now houses the Civic Museum with Roman antiquities and other historic material.

A long stairway, Via delle Mura Ciclopiche, descends from the Piazza della Signoria, past stretches of the pre-Roman walls, to the lower sections of Spoleto. Of the several churches around town the most interesting, besides the cathedral, is the Romanesque edifice of San Gregorio Maggiore off the Piazza Garibaldi on the low northern outskirts. Dedicated to a local martyr, it was erected in the eleventh century on the spot where, near the "sanguinary" bridge (p. 93), according to a Latin inscription, 10,000 victims of the anti-Christian persecutions were buried. Much-damaged frescoes from the twelfth to the fifteenth centuries can be seen in the church's stark interior above a large crypt.

Three other churches in the surroundings of Spoleto are also noteworthy. San Pietro, on the slopes of Monteluco (p. 102), may be reached in a twenty-minute walk from the upper town. Medieval sculptures in panels on its facade develop themes of ancient bestiaries—the fox preaching to the sheep; the fox feigning death; a defenseless man imploring a lion to spare him; an armed man fighting a lion; and other incidents.

San Salvatore, standing on a terrace within Spoleto's cemetery on the city's northern outskirts off the Via Flaminia (National Route No. 3) near the turnoff to Norcia, is a weather-bitten early-Christian basilica. It dates from the fourth or fifth century, incorporating Doric columns and other fragments from a vanished pagan temple. Nearby, on higher ground, is the thirteenth-century Church of San Ponziano with medieval frescoes by minor Umbrian painters; adjacent is a monastery of Augustinian nuns.

⌁ A Sacred Mountain ⌁

Arriving in Spoleto by whatever means and route you travel, your first impression will probably be the stern hilltop fortress and the mountain ridge that provides a dark green backdrop for it and the city. The Citadel, which the Spoletans simply call La Rocca (the stronghold), is visible from many points in the city. Built between 1362 and 1370, it is the most imposing of the many military structures that the imperious, cunning, and able Cardinal Albornoz scattered in Umbria.

No visitor to Spoleto should omit taking a stroll on the roads around the castle hill. Start at the Piazza Campello, east of the cathedral, and proceed on the Via del Ponte, named after the spectacular high bridge that is a city landmark (p. 101), to return by way of the Via della Rocca and Via M. Gattapone, with good views of the cathedral, the city, and the Spoleto plain. The main gate to the fortress compound is above the Piazza Campello.

La Rocca is a lengthy, rectangular complex, 426 feet by 108 feet, with six towers and two large courtyards. Through the centuries popes, papal governors, generals, troops, and prisoners lived in it. Among its inhabitants was Lucrezia Borgia, the beautiful and scandal-prone daughter of Pope Alexander VI, in 1499 when she was named by him governor of Spoleto and Foligno. She was then nineteen years old, a pawn in the manipulative hands of her father and her ruthless brother Cesare Borgia, and was soon to be a widow again: Her second husband, Alfonso of Aragon, would be assassinated in the Vatican next year on orders, probably, from the nefarious Cesare. Inevitably, the Spoletans to this day tell fantastic stories about a lustful Lucrezia having her occasional lovers hurled down the walls and cliffs of the fortress at the end of an amorous night.

After serving for centuries as a principal seat of papal government in the region, the Citadel saw again military action in 1860. In the course of Italy's unification the forces of Sardinia-Piedmont had advanced into Umbria and besieged the Spoleto stronghold. It was defended by an Irish brigade in Pope Pius IX's service, commanded by Major Myles W. P. O'Reilly, but after two days of fighting with casualties on either side it had to surrender.

The fortress became again a penitentiary (which it had been during the last few decades of papal rule), and remained one until the 1980s. Spoletans told me that quite a few of the inmates during their long terms learned such trades as pottery or woodwork. In a setting of great natural beauty and above a town steeped in art, the prisoners were encouraged to shape pleasing objects with their hands, although there must have always been the danger that they might use their tools for attacks on the guards or break-out attempts.

The old papal Citadel no longer houses prisoners. The cells into which its large halls had been subdivided early in the nineteenth century have been demolished, and when I last was in Spoleto the interior of La Rocca was still being restructured while the sandblasted outer walls looked like new—too bright for my taste and for that of many Spoletans to whom I spoke. I had my suspicions that local promoters had not yet given up their plan to install a gambling casino in the once-grim complex, although the national Parliament had just voted down a motion that would have authorized a few more such places in addition to four legal gaming establishments that were then functioning in Italy. Officially, the readapted fortress was still destined to become a cultural institution and convention center.

A deep ravine between the fortress hill and the mountain behind it, Monteluco, is spanned by an audacious bridge. This tall structure, known as the Bridge of the Towers, rises 266 feet above the deepest point of the gorge, is 251 yards in length, and serves as both a viaduct and an aqueduct, resting on ten arches. Cardinal Albornoz requested his able architect, Matteo di Giovanello, called Gattapone, from Gubbio (circa 1300–1383), the builder of La Rocca, to supply the Citadel with water; the bold bridge was Gattapone's solution. He used the remnants of earlier constructions because the ravine had been bridged, though at lesser height, since ancient Roman times.

Gattapone's bridge is open to pedestrians. A window midway permits a look into the abyss, and it is from here that suicides from time to time jump to their deaths. "It's curious," a Spoletan remarked to me, "that they always leave their shoes behind on the floor of the bridge. Perhaps it's easier to climb barefoot up to the window to squeeze through and leap."

It may be just an urban legend, but I was told by local people that when La Rocca was still a penitentiary, the convicts, looking out of the cells and common rooms of their lofty jail, were often the first to report that the body of yet another suicide was lying in the deep gorge below them. I have even heard tales of the prison inmates managing to save one or the other death candidate who had suspiciously lingered on the bridge; if they alerted their wardens and quick action was taken, the would-be suicide could be prevented from jumping.

Gattapone's 600-year-old daunting stone bridge links the fortress hill with the western slope of the Monteluco, Spoleto's "Holy Mountain." Its Italian name is derived from the Latin word *lucus,* meaning sacred grove. A dense coat of ilex shrubs and evergreen oaks with dark, leathery leaves wraps the limestone ridge.

In antiquity it was forbidden to cut wood on the mountain because its forest was considered to be hallowed. Spoleto's Civic Museum (p. 98) treasures two stone markers from the third century B.C., which are inscribed in archaic Latin with the so-called *lex spoletina* (Spoletan law), establishing sanctions for violating the ban: Whoever took wood not destined for religious uses must sacrifice an ox to Jupiter and pay a fine. A modern replica of the markers with the Latin text and an Italian translation stands among the trees on the flat summit of the Monteluco.

The notion of sanctity clung to the mountain also in the early Christian era. Syrian anchorites retired to it, and their hermitage on a slope survived for many centuries until its last occupants were evicted at the time of the French Revolution. Today their empty, primitive limestone abode can be visited.

It takes ninety minutes to two hours to climb Monteluco on a footpath starting at the eastern end of the Bridge of the Towers. A paved road winds in many bends from the Piazza Campello almost to the top of Monteluco, which is 2,723 feet above sea level and 1,400 feet above the city. The principal sight on the summit is the Franciscan convent.

St. Francis of Assisi loved the Monteluco, and near its highest point founded one of his first monasteries, adjacent to an already existing Benedictine chapel. The seven low and narrow cells of his friars and a water well in the courtyard are still visible. The poor Franciscan construction consisted of tree branches forming walls covered with plaster on either side and protected by a rudimentary roof. St. Bernardine of Siena (p. 47) who in 1430 spent some time in the little convent had the building strengthened and expanded. Today the cells of the first friars are roofed with brown tiles, and there is a low bell tower of rough stones.

Masses are said and devotions held daily in the oft-restored chapel, which now has dark brown wood paneling. Under a side altar are the remains of the Blessed Leopoldo da Gaiche (1732–1815), a Franciscan missionary who for many years lived in the little Monteluco monastery. Outside the chapel, on a white-washed wall, an Italian inscription reads:

> *If you believe, pray*
> *If you don't believe, admire*
> *If you are a fool, write your name on the wall.*

There are no graffiti.

Michelangelo visited the Monteluco hermitage and the monastery in 1556 and was enchanted by the scenery. The best vantage point is a stone belvedere a few hundred yards from the Franciscan convent; nearby now are a huge steel cross and a television and telecommunications mast. The panorama encompasses the city of Spoleto below and an ample segment of Umbria's hills and valleys with, afar, Assisi, Perugia, and Gubbio.

The broad summit of Monteluco is meticulously clean; a detachment of the Forest Guard, a specialized national police force, sees to it that the many excursionists, campers, and sightseers who ascend the mountain respect the beautiful environment. Wooden tables for picnickers are near fountains spilling Monteluco's famed water (which also supplies the city below and its hilltop fortress). Several villas stand amid the forests in various spots on the slopes, but it seems that the city of Spoleto, whose territory includes Monteluco, issues no further permits to build on it. A large children's home and a couple of hotels named "Paradiso" and "Hermitage" are near the old Franciscan monastery.

Take a walk at the foot of the Monteluco or elsewhere in Spoleto's wooded surroundings, and you will soon notice signs, TRUFFLE HUNTING PROHIBITED. This modern version of the ancient Spoletan law (p. 102) indicates truffle cultivations. Under a national law of 1985 anyone may search for truffles that occur wild, but areas in which the tubers are being cultivated are protected from outsiders. Of course, illegal truffle hunting is nevertheless going on all the time.

Some animals, especially pigs and dogs, are particularly sensitive to the smell of truffles—which to human noses often seems faint—and will dig them out of the earth. In Umbria, trained dogs are generally used for tracing the aromatic fungi; start giving a whelp a choice morsel of sausage or cake whenever it finds a truffle, and it will soon become an accomplished helpmate in harvesting the annual crop. Such collaboration between master and dog appears to have been going on for thousands of years. The few wild boars that still roam the hills in the area love truffles and dig them up on their own for their dinner.

The ancient Greeks, Libyans, and Romans liked truffles on their tables; Pliny the Elder, in his *Natural History*, correctly classified the delicacy as a plant, whereas other writers of his epoch tended to assign them to mineralogy or to the animal kingdom.

In Umbria truffles occur between one and two feet below the soil surface, are of irregular shape, and are between a walnut and an apple in size. They grow in symbiosis with certain trees, especially oaks, and are usually associated with their roots; their relationship with their host plant is intricate. In the Spoleto area the black truffle species (often with whitish veins in the dark flesh) prevails; in the Norcia and Gubbio districts many truffles are white or yellowish. Umbrian connoisseurs seem divided as to which color, shape, and size of the fungi are preferable. Black truffles mature in autumn or early winter, whites a little later in winter.

Truffles appear to have been used in cooking in Umbria since antiquity. Cultivation of the plant in the region by seeding appropriate woodland with acorns or by other techniques is much younger. Toward the end of the nineteenth century French merchants became interested in Umbria's truffle potential, and propagated cultivating the fungi in that region. (The tubers had long been systematically grown in the *truffières* of the Périgord and other parts of France.) Today truffle culture and conservation is an Umbrian industry, competing with truffle producers in the neighboring Marche region and especially in Piedmont in northwestern Italy. A sizable portion of the Umbrian output is exported, mainly to France, Germany, and the United States.

In Umbria itself, many restaurants offer truffles as a seasoning for pasta or meat every day. In Spoleto the kind of noodles known

as *strangozzi* (p. xiii) often come with black truffles. Another
Spoleto specialty is omelet with sliced or crushed black truffles
and sprinkled with lemon juice.

◡ *Witchcraft and Sausages* ◡

If you aren't rushed, it is a good idea to devote at least a day to a
side trip from Spoleto to Norcia—and maybe also to Cascia—
before proceeding to Assisi. My latest visit to that offbeat eastern
salient of Umbria was with a Spoletan and an American. It was a
sunny late-autumn day, and as we were driving up National Route
No. 395 toward the Forca di Cerro, a 2,350-foot-high pass
between the valleys of two mountain streams, the New Yorker
exclaimed: "Just look! It's better than the fall foliage in New
England!"

The short oaks, ilexes, and shrubs on the hillsides all around
composed a palette of browns, reds, and dark greens. The well-
kept highway was all ours for long stretches; at one point where
it descends to a gully of the Nera River the blue public bus that
shuttles between Norcia and the railroad station of Spoleto
crossed us. You cannot travel by rail to Norcia anymore. A high
viaduct and several tunnels, all unused today, are remnants of the
narrow-gauge electric railway that once linked the two cities. I
remember that on my first visit the train took more than two
hours for the thirty-two-mile distance, but I loved every minute of
it because of the magnificent Apennine panorama of cliffs,
ravines, dark forests, gray clusters of stone houses perched on
peaks and ridges like eagle nests, and snow-capped high mountains on the eastern horizon. Train service on the unprofitable line
was discontinued in 1968.

During that train ride many years ago I was impressed by the intense blue of the Nera's waters in its upper reaches. Now I was gratified to see that they still had that color. The Nera is Umbria's second river next to the "blond" Tiber, whose tributary it is. An old adage, which in the local dialect rhymes, says, "The Tiber wouldn't be the Tiber if the Nera didn't give it to drink." The two rivers join near Orte, the road and rail hub close to the border between the Umbria and Latium regions. Today the waters of the Nera, usually more copious than those of the Tiber, are harnessed by more than twenty hydroelectric plants along its seventy-two-mile course.

The first time I visited Norcia wasn't out of piety aroused by St. Benedict, who was born there, but because of curiosity about the district's reputation for witchcraft. I had first learned of it through a passage in Benvenuto Cellini's *Autobiography* (I, 65): The Florentine artist, jeweler and adventurer tells of his dealings with a sorcerer, a Sicilian priest who attempts to ensnare him in magic practices. In the ruined Colosseum in Rome the priest "arrayed himself in a necromancer's robes, began to describe circles on the earth," and burned perfumes on a fire, claiming to have summoned legions of devils. When Cellini shows interest in being further initiated, the priest tells him that the most suitable locality for the purpose is "the hill country of Norcia" and that the peasants there "are people to be trusted, and have some practice in these, matters." As it happens, Cellini is too busy with other things to pursue black magic.

Later I had read in Jakob Burckhardt's classic, *The Civilization of the Renaissance in Italy* (VI), of persistent rumors that "at Norcia, the home of St. Benedict, there was a perfect nest of witches and sorcerers; no secret was made of it." Burckhardt quotes from a letter by Aeneas Sylvius, the later Pope Pius II (1405–64), to his brother: "Not far from the town of Norcia there is a cave beneath a steep rock in which water flows. There, as I remember to have heard, are witches, demons and nightly shades, and he that has the courage can see and speak to ghosts, and learn magic arts."

When, during my first visit, I asked a few people in Norcia about *stregoneria* (witchcraft) I got first blank stares and then indulgent smiles; maybe the young foreigner was thought to be crazy or the credulous butt of some jokester.

Since then I have heard repeatedly that belief in sorcery stubbornly endures in some corners of Umbria. If a small child in some village seems forever sickly and the doctor doesn't know what to do about it, old women will tell the mother the infant has been hexed, and the only possible cure is a tea made by boiling "witches' herbs," various weeds growing wildly. Such superstition lingers in various rural parts of Italy, as do faith in love potions and fear of the "evil eye."

During my recent series of visits in Umbria I was astonished to learn that "satanic cults" had found followers in some places there. One story was that a group of well-to-do people was meeting in a lonely villa near the industrial city of Terni to celebrate black masses—adoration of Satan in a travesty of Roman Catholic liturgy. Similar reports came also from other districts in the country; police investigated rumors about Satanism in the hillside south of Rome, suspecting that the alleged episodes of devil worship were covers for drug parties or prostitution rackets. On my latest trip to Norcia, as during earlier ones, I speculated again which of the wild gullies in the city's surroundings may have been a witches' lair.

The last few miles of our car trip we passed a long road tunnel and, eventually, less than an hour after our departure from Spoleto, looked down on Norcia in what seemed a hollow, but actually is a plateau, 1,982 feet above sea level. In the east we saw the Sibillini Range, or Mountains of the Sibyl. Was the Sibyl, the prophetess of ancient myth after which the mountain chain is named, a sorceress? The Sibillini mountains, now a national park, mark here the border between Umbria and the Region of the Marches on the Adriatic side of the Italian peninsula. The highest peak visible from Norcia, the 4,911-foot Monte Fusconi, was already wearing a bonnet of snow.

We parked our car outside the yellow-gray stone walls, which were first erected 2,000 years ago and over the centuries were continually repaired, strengthened, and extended. Today they are 6,900 feet long, with seventeen towers and eight gates, enclosing all of historic Norcia. Some 2,000 people still live within the ancient fortifications, and a little more than that number in modern suburbs in the plain all around them.

We penetrated the old town through its main entrance, the massive Roman Gate, which, despite its classical name, was built only in 1869. On the outside it bears the large Latin inscription VETUSTA NURSIA—Ancient Norcia. When the Romans conquered the town in 290 B.C. they took over its archaic name, Nursia, which may have been derived from a pre-Roman goddess (or a witch, again?) who was venerated here.

The Roman Gate opens into a straight main street, 275 yards long, cutting through the western part of town toward its religious and civic center, St. Benedict's Square. The street was laid out after a disastrous earthquake in 1859, which killed a hundred people and caused many buildings to collapse. The subsoil is treacherous in the Norcia basin; the town was afflicted by catastrophic quakes in the eighteenth century, and there was again a strong tremor in 1979, during which works of art in its museum were damaged. Most structures in Norcia are no taller than three stories.

Dignified nineteenth-century houses line the principal street, which isn't too large. It was very clean when we visited the town, and I recalled the general neatness that had struck me here also on earlier occasions. The main drag is called Corso Sertorio in honor of a Norcia native, Quintus Sertorius (122–72 B.C.), the Roman general who at one time was master of most of Spain, but failed to prevail upon his enemies in Rome and was assassinated by one of his own men.

Right and left of the Roman Gate's inner side are two similar buildings, either one an outpost of the Italian state: the Carabinieri station and the post office. Next to them are abundantly stocked shops selling the products of the local food industry for which Norcia today is far better known nationwide than it is for presumed witchcraft. "Sausages, not sorcery!" I couldn't help saying, causing my companions to wince with exaggeration. The show windows and store shelves were bulging with hams, salami, cheeses, black and white truffles, and peasant bread as well as little white loaves artistically arranged in flower patterns. A small hunk of pork meat carried the label "portable ham"; a salami specialty was marked with the vulgar name of a jackass's organs of generation.

Norcia has for centuries been famous for its pork specialties; in Rome as elsewhere in central Italy a store selling ham, salami, and kindred eatables is today still known as a *norcineria*. And the *norcino*, the bluff and pretendedly naïve pork butcher from Norcia, was one of the stock characters of Roman popular comedy in the seventeenth and eighteenth centuries.

✌ Patron of Europe ✍

In the Piazza San Benedetto at the end of Corso Sertorio stands a white marble statue of St. Benedict by the Sicilian sculptor Francesco Prinzi that was put up there in 1880, the fourteenth centenary of the saint's birth. On the left side of the square are the medieval Town Hall and the Church of St. Benedict, which goes back to the early Middle Ages; on the right are the sixteenth-century cathedral and a stout little Renaissance fortress called the Castellina (little castle), now home of the Civic Museum.

The irregularly shaped, almost circular square, from which nine streets and lanes radiate like the spokes of a wheel, is esthetically most satisfying. In my judgment it belongs to the best in a country that is enviably rich in impressive urban spaces. It doesn't disturb at all—on the contrary, it enlives the architectural frame—that hams, salami, cheeses, and truffles are displayed by stores all around the square.

The Church of St. Benedict is at the spot where, according to tradition, the founder of the Benedictine Order and his twin sister, St. Scholastica, were born around A.D. 480. A sanctuary was erected here already in the sixth century; it was completely rebuilt in A.D. 1389, and repaired and altered several times later. The fourteenth-century facade, with sculptured ornamentation, is flanked by statuettes of the twin saints in two recesses and surmounted by a Gothic relief sculpture of the Virgin Mary between two angels. Below the gable is a large rose window.

The austere single nave of the church's interior is decorated with frescoes and paintings from various epochs, some representing scenes from the life of St. Benedict. He was proclaimed Patron Saint of Europe by Pope Pius XII in 1958, the year when the

European Common Market, forerunner of the European Union, was established under the Treaty of Rome.

Two staircases descend to the crypt built into the ruins of a Roman house that may or may not have been the birthplace of St. Benedict and his sister St. Scholastica. The father of the twins, identified as Euproprius of the prominent Anicii family, is believed to have been a magistrate. Excavations begun before World War I brought to light the remains of walls suggesting that what once stood there was an official Roman building; scholars speculate that the twin saints' father may indeed have served as a functionary in it but that his family lived elsewhere, maybe in the area outside the present city where the Church of St. Scholastica (p. 116) was later built.

The crypt is divided into three rectangular, vaulted rooms; one ends in a niche with a little altar where, according to legend, the saintly twins actually entered the world. Patches of fourteenth-century frescoes depicting episodes from the two saints' later lives are still visible. An iron grille at one end of the crypt allows the visitor to look into an archeological site where remains of stout Roman brickwork have been dug up. Present-day devotees throw coins across the bars of the grille into the excavations as into a wishing well.

Benedict spent only his childhood years in Nursia (Norcia), it seems. His father sent him to school in Rome, but the young student, said to have been soon disgusted by the dolce vita he found there, fled and became a hermit in the mountain wilderness near Subiaco, fifty-five miles south of his birthplace. He founded twelve monasteries there, giving them his rule *ora et labora* (pray and work). When he got into trouble with the jealous local clergy, he moved to the rock of Montecassino, eighty miles south of

Rome, where he founded the first abbey of his order. His sister, St. Scholastica, followed him and established a nunnery two miles distant from the abbey.

St. Gregory—who as Pope Gregory I (590–604) was revered as Gregory the Great—reports that the King of the Ostrogoths, Totila, visited St. Benedict shortly before the latter's death in A.D. 547. St. Scholastica died, according to tradition, forty days before her brother; both are buried in Montecassino. The abbey on the rock was destroyed in a 1944 battle, and soon after World War II was rebuilt—for the fourth time in its 1,400-year history.

Leaving the Church of St. Benedict, we looked into the portico along its right outer wall, and I noticed that the big stone measures for grain that I remembered from earlier visits were still there. The porch was added to the church by the local authorities in 1570, despite protests from the Benedictine monks, for a mundane purpose: to provide a covered cereal market for the town. The massive, square clock tower behind the mercantile portico was originally much taller; it was shortened, and the stump reinforced, after earth tremors in the eighteenth century had damaged it.

Past the shop windows with their hams and truffles we stepped to the cathedral. A much less interesting and distinguished building than the Church of St. Benedict, it was erected in the sixteenth century and dedicated to the Virgin Mary in memory of a long-lost, supposedly miraculous, silver image of the Madonna. The broad facade is plain, the campanile at its right side sturdy. Inside, the art work in the three naves isn't outstanding. There is a marble bust of Pope John Paul II over an inscription recording that the Polish pontiff visited Norcia in March 1980 to mark the fifteen hundredth anniversary of St. Benedict's birth and to bring comfort to the townspeople who had endured another earthquake a few months earlier. John Paul II addressed the assembled clergy of the Spoleto-Norcia Archdiocese in the cathedral on that occasion.

We walked from the cathedral to the Castellina, hoping to view the renowned terra-cotta Annunciation by Andrea della Robbia of Florence, and the sculptures and paintings from the fourteenth and fifteenth centuries in Norcia's Civic Museum. However, we found locked doors: The institution had remained closed since the earthquake of 1979, and although most of the damaged walls and exhibits had meanwhile been repaired, not one of the six showrooms had been reopened. So we looked at the outside of the stern, square building with its four corner towers. It was designed by no less an architect than Vignola (whose real name was Jacopo Barozzi), Michelangelo's successor in the long-drawn-out construction of St. Peter's in Rome.

The Castellina wasn't really meant as a fortress but as the fortified residence of the papal governors of the town and district. Pope Julius III had the nonmilitary stronghold erected, as a Latin inscription on the north tower explains, after "local tumults" in 1554 when the townspeople rebelled against the authorities. Papal officials in Umbria had their problems.

During my first visit to Norcia the frowning Castellina was the courthouse and seat of other government offices. Later it was transformed into a district museum where all major works of art in the churches of the city and of the villages around it were to be gathered; however, the clergy and the congregations of some churches clung to the Madonnas and other revered paintings and would not surrender them to the museum. After the 1979 earthquake some works of art that had been yielded were returned, at least temporarily, to the places whence they had been taken.

We completed our tour of Norcia's main square in front of the Town Hall. This is a cream-colored building that goes back to the fourteenth century, was damaged by various earthquakes, and was almost totally rebuilt 120 years ago, complete with a squat clock tower and a loggia. Two nineteenth-century stone lions flanking an outside staircase were clearly inspired by Antonio Canova, the classical revivalist of the Napoleonic era.

There were at least half a dozen more churches with their Madonnas, frescoes, and other art to see, but we just walked by the fourteenth-century Church of San Francesco, a few steps north of the Castellina. The plainness of the Gothic edifice, which looks like a huge container made of gray stone, is relieved by a remarkable rose window in its facade.

A sign indicating the way to the Tempietto (little temple) on the upper side of the city prompted us to climb up there. On a street corner we found a massive little stone structure, maybe twenty feet high, with unframed, glassless windows and richly ornamented, round arches under a red-tiled roof. "None of our earthquakes has ever been able to shake this," said an elderly man who from a doorway watched us as we were gazing at the Tempietto. "A local stonecutter built it six hundred years ago; he sure knew how to make it quake-proof." And what was the Tempietto supposed to mean? Our informant looked quizzical: "Nobody knows for sure. Probably the Tempietto served as a shelter for a Madonna statue; there are still traces of frescoes inside, but they are very faded. Or maybe it was built to keep a pledge made during a plague."

At this point the three of us were hungry, and we were told that the Taverna del Boscaiolo (The Woodcutter's Tavern) was the place for getting a decent meal. To reach it, we passed Norcia's dignified Civic Theater, with a red and yellow neoclassical facade. Unlike other old playhouses in the region, Norcia's theater hasn't become a cinema, but occasionally still stages dramas and even operas, performed by semiprofessional troupes.

The Woodcutter's Tavern turned out to be a cozy basement place with a computer in a little, open office, but also with a genuine wood fire in the very clean kitchen. After a hot and homely spelt soup (*minestra di farro*) we couldn't say no to the house specialty, a big platter of grilled pork sausages and cuts of lamb and veal. The house wine was red and strong. "Sagrantino of Montefalco, of course," said the blond woman, possibly the manager, who served us.

A siesta would have been the right sequel to such a lunch, but we had more sight-seeing on our program. Driving on a straight, level road for a little more than a mile, we reached the Church of St. Scholastica near the place where the twin sister of St. Benedict is supposed to have lived until she joined him in Montecassino. Today the simple church, in part rebuilt in the eighteenth century, is adjacent to Norcia's cemetery. On the inside walls are large patches of badly damaged frescoes from the sixteenth century representing episodes of St. Benedict's life. Visitors have covered the church's interior with graffiti during 500 years—signatures, coats of arms, invocations of saints, avowals of very earthly love, crosses, stars, and even swastikas.

✧ Saint of the Impossible ✧

We wanted to have a look also at Cascia in the hills southwest of Norcia. We returned to the last stretch of the way we had come, and at the village of Serravalle turned south on National Route

No. 320, which through gorges and around many bends mounts the valley of the Corno stream. Ruins of two medieval strongholds on rocky spurs left and right contribute to the romantic scenery.

Cascia, less than eight miles south of Serravalle, has had a long and often turbulent history, but to Italians its name is indissolubly linked with that of St. Rita, widely revered as the "saint of the impossible." When the physicians say there is no hope, the patient who has been given up by medical science, or the sick person's relatives, will undertake a pilgrimage to Cascia to pray for a miraculous recovery. Many come in wheelchairs. And married couples whose wish for a child has been disappointed year after year will be told: "Pray to St. Rita!"

The Rev. Giustino Casciano, rector of the Cascia sanctuary, said: "There are a great many couples who, it seems, can't have babies. St. Rita has helped many of them." The rector, in the black garb of the Augustinian fathers, added: "Many of the devout people who come here suffer from serious illnesses, some in the terminal stage. Every day someone tells us they have received the grace of getting better." The sanctuary's files contain hundreds of testimonials expressing gratitude to St. Rita, often in naïve phrases, "for grace received."

The saint who is credited with such power in heaven was Margherita Lotti (1381–circa 1447). A native of a mountain hamlet above Cascia, she got married in Cascia. After her husband was slain, either in a feud or by bandits, and their two children, in their teens, had died too, Margherita, or Rita, entered a local Benedictine convent at the age of thirty-six. Her piety and charitableness became proverbial, and after her death many miracles, attributed to her intercession with God, were reported. The

Vatican proclaimed her "Blessed" in 1628; Pope Leo XIII canonized her in 1900.

The cult of St. Rita has long been Cascia's principal source of income as pilgrims have continued to flock to the town to pray for "impossible" mercies. The saint's tomb is in an imposing church halfway up the hill on which Cascia spreads. This new Basilica of St. Rita, consecrated in 1947, is an edifice of bright travertine stone in which Byzantine and Romanesque style motifs are mixed in a twentieth-century medley. The facade between two low front towers with conical roofs displays a large cross flanked by angels in a relief under a curved window; the rectangular portal underneath is bordered by bas-relief panels with scenes from the saint's life. The church's interior is profuse with marble; its Chapel of St. Rita shelters the saint's mummified remains.

A modern, arcaded twin loggia in front of the church is often filled with devotees shuffling to the sanctuary while saying prayers. Hotels, pilgrims' hostels, eating places, and souvenir shops are all over town. Conscientious sightseers would have visited also the former convent of St. Rita as well as a couple of old churches, the ruins of a Roman temple, and the hulk of a fifteenth-century fortress, but we had seen enough for the day. We got strong espressos at a coffee bar near the sanctuary to reinvigorate us for the seventy-minute drive back to Spoleto.

4

⌣∴∾

The Road to Assisi II

Drive north from Spoleto on the Via Flaminia (National Route No. 3) through a tunnel under the fortress hill and for another twelve miles to reach one of Umbria's most famous spots, the Source of the Clitumnus River (Fonti del Clitunno).

Whenever I revisited it, I would invariably observe groups of tourists standing around under the poplars and the weeping willows, staring into the round pond of clear water and the little grassy islands in it, and then looking at one another as if to ask, "Is that all?"

They had been brought by bus from Rome, Spoleto, or Assisi, and were promised to be shown a place that Virgil and Byron, among many other greats, had praised. They had been traveling

on the busy highway, crossing a plain cluttered with modern residential buildings, small factories, service stations, motels, and
what seemed a few run-down former farmsteads. Their tour bus
had parked outside a fenced enclave with trees rustling in the
breeze. Now, inside, after gazing for a while at the swans and
ducks in the water, the visitors would head for the refreshment
and souvenir stand. Ten minutes later they would be on the bus
again, probably still wondering what their sight-seeing stop was
supposed to be all about.

"There is nothing that doesn't cause delight," wrote Pliny the
Younger to a friend after he had at last been at the source of the
Clitumnus, "and I am sorry it was so late." He described the pure,
cold water that was so clear that one could see every single peb-
ble on the bottom as well as the coins that had been dropped into
it. The trees around the pool were reflected in the water, and an
ancient, venerated temple stood nearby.

The younger Pliny, as an imperial jurist and official, had seen a
good many illustrious spots in Italy and outside the peninsula; he
nevertheless was at once struck by the source of the Clitumnus. I
confess that when I first saw it on a trip to the Adriatic I had the
feeling I just didn't get what was so exceptional about the site. As
we were walking back to the car outside the fence, I had trouble
explaining to my little son Ernesto why we had stopped. "Well,
Carducci wrote an ode about the Fonti del Clitunno, and sooner
or later you'll learn in school about it, and you will be able to tell
the teacher you have seen the place," I lamely told him.

Giosuè Carducci visited the landmark in 1876 when he was
acting as government inspector of the high school in nearby
Spoleto, and the "pure source" inspired one of his most solemn

poems. A marble marker close to the pond with the relief of a dancing faun and nymphs recalls Carducci's visit.

There is no memorial for Byron, although he too, and earlier, had celebrated the spot:

> *Clitumnus, in thy sweetest wave*
> *Of the most living crystal that was e'er*
> *The haunt of river nymphs to gaze and lave*
> *Her limbs where nothing hid them thou doest rear*
> *Thy grassy banks . . .*
>
> —CHILDE HAROLD (IV, 66)

Byron traveled across Umbria in 1817, and at the source of Clitumnus found the "gentle waters . . . most serene of aspect, and most clear."

To appreciate the beauty of the scenery, whose serenity is unusual today, one needs leisure. A ten-minute stop on the tour itinerary plainly isn't enough. You must let the calm, the soft lines of the landscape, the twitter of the birds in the trees around the cool, transparent pond sink in. The beauty of the spot grows on you. So close to the much-traveled highway and the Rome-Ancona railroad line, the Source of Clitumnus is a little realm of timeless calm.

To the ancient Umbrians it was a sacred place, and the Romans revered it too. Virgil and Propertius mention in their poetry that animals were purified in the Clitumnus before being sacrificed to the gods. Suetonius reports that Emperor Caligula (A.D. 37–41) visited the "River Clitumnus and its sacred grove," apparently to ask an oracle to reveal the future to him. Pliny the Younger in his letter from the Clitumnus informed his friend that the river god had an ancient temple there, and that he was "benignant and prophetic"; shrines of other deities too were scattered in the area, covered with a multitude of graffiti, "some of which will make you smile." According to Pliny, the stream flowing out of the clear pond could be navigated, and had such a broad bed that two boats being rowed in opposite directions could pass each other.

It seems that an earthquake in A.D. 440 diminished the volume of water. The sources below the surface of the shallow pond nevertheless have remained very productive, yielding today an average of more than 400 gallons per second. In the Middle Ages the towns of Trevi and Montefalco, east and west of the river, were for centuries quarreling over use of its copious water output until they reached a compromise in a formal treaty in 1315. At present the Clitumnus, by way of several canals, waters the fertile plain, and joins the Topino River northwest of Foligno to contribute to the Cascio and eventually to the Tiber.

The weeping willows that, together with the poplars, surround the source of the Clitumnus were brought there in 1865 from St. Helena, the Atlantic island where Napoleon died in 1821, as a tribute to the French emperor, regarded as a champion of Italian unity.

A little less than a mile downstream from the source stands the so-called Tempietto, or little temple, of Clitumnus, actually a church. It was built on a modest hill in the early fifth century with material from pagan sanctuaries; its four elegant Corinthian columns face the stream and an old mill. Traces of frescoes from the seventh century inside are the oldest Christian paintings existing anywhere in Umbria.

To Byron the temple-chapel was a seal of Clitumnus's blessings:

And on thy lappy shore a Temple still
Of small and delicate proportions keeps
Upon a mild declivity of hill
Its memory of thee; beneath it sweeps
Thy current's calmness; oft from out it leaps
The finny darter with the glittering scales
Who dwells and revels in thy glassy deeps;
While, chance, some scattered water lily sails
Down where the shallower wave still tells its bubbling tales.

If the scene provides respite from "weary life," Byron con-
cluded, it is to Clitumnus that

Ye must
Pay orisons for this suspension of disgust.

—*CHILDE HAROLD* (*IV, 68*)

⌁ *Oil Town* ⌁

Another couple of miles northward the traveler is greeted at a
turnoff by a sign carrying an olive-shaped blotch of dark green
and the words CITTÀ DELL'OLIVO (Olive City). A steep road
curves up between terraced olive groves to small, neat Trevi, 600
feet above its railroad station and the national highway. A much-
photographed place, walled Trevi climbs in the shape of a shell—
its right side broader than the left—on a nearly perfect cone.

The graceful town of 7,500 people wants to be recognized as the capital of olive oil, although in this respect it has many rivals in Umbria and in other Italian regions from Sicily to Liguria. During my latest visit I saw posters urging the citizenry to attend a public debate on a project to establish a Museum of Olive Oil Civilization in Trevi. A restaurant a little outside the walls simply calls itself L'Ulivo (The Olive).

In November and December one can see lines of people, hemp bags strapped to their chests or dangling from their necks, plucking the green fruits from the trees that are Trevi's chief asset and assure its well-being. Each laborer carries a hook for catching the higher branches, and drops the olives into the bag, which is kept open by a wooden hoop. In the olive groves of Trevi as elsewhere in Umbria most of the harvesting is still done by hand. Beating the fruits from the branches with sticks damages both the crop and the tree, and mechanical methods to bring in the fruits are being introduced only hesitantly.

Olive plucking isn't really hard work, but because of the autumn chills and humidity or rains it may become tedious. Farmers told me of the old times when groups of people, known as companies, harvesting olives on some slope under the supervision of a foreman, would challenge one another with songs to produce the day's largest yield. Today, landowners have trouble getting enough hands for olive garnering; they hire African migrant workers to do the job, or let students earn some money (off the books, of course) by plucking olives instead of attending classes at Perugia University.

Modern oil mills and storehouses spread in the Clitunno Valley at the foot of Trevi. Old-timers still remember small hillside mills powered by horses or mules that were driven with their eyes bandaged to prevent giddiness. The olives were crushed by the mill stones and then put under presses. The liquid yielded by the first pressing has since oldest times been known as virgin oil; marketing hype has long invented the term *extra vérgine*, claiming a superior degree of virginity for the first product.

One of the ancient rites of olive culture consists of testing the newly pressed oil by spreading it together with salt and a little garlic on slices of fresh bread toasted over a wood fire. The simple snack is known as bruschetta, literally "little brush." It has been a favorite appetizer in Umbrian eating places as long as I have known them, and lately has become fashionable also in pretentious restaurants throughout Italy. To eat bruschetta in an Umbrian oil mill (a *frantoio*), washing it down with local wine, is, of course, the real thing. In Trevi all taverns serve bruschetta and wine on the Feast of Immaculate Conception, December 8, when the town celebrates its new oil.

Another traditional celebration in Trevi is the Celery Festival in October. It has an erotic subtext: Celery is considered an aphrodisiac all over Italy, and the dark variety of the plant grown around Trevi is supposed to be particularly powerful. It seems that semipagan customs, like a spinsters' procession to the Church of Santa Maria di Pietraressa outside the town to pray for husbands, were connected with the celery harvest. Pope Gregory XIII (1572–85), who had long lived in Umbria before his elevation to the pontifical throne, prohibited the devotion; he knew about its thinly veiled significance. The purported properties of Trevi's celery may be a reason why that town's men, the *trevigiani*, have a reputation as lotharios all over the region.

The annual celery festival coincides with a traditional race in which four burly youths of each of Trevi's three town districts (the *terzieri*) push a cart to the town's watchtower while a fifth man is steering the vehicle. The contest, passionately followed by the residents of the *terzieri*, scarcely lasts more than two minutes.

Trevi, however, is also more sophisticated than that. During a recent visit I found that its small, neoclassical Clitunno Theater, built in 1875, had just received a fresh coat of beige and red paint, and that it was rehearsing a production of Federico Garcia Lorca's *The House of Bernarda Alba*. The Spanish poet and dramatist's last completed play (before Franco's soldiers shot him) requires Bernarda's five unmarried daughters and three other women on the stage; the town whose spinsters' race was once found indecent by a pope was going to be treated now to a theatrical show about virginity, frustration, and family honor.

Near the theater is Trevi's three-story Town Hall with a low, almost oppressive arcade. The building is from the fourteenth century, as is the four-sided watchtower to its right. A small picture gallery on the second floor of the mayor's office contains one of several Coronation of Mary paintings by Lo Spagna and other works by the Spoletan master. Lo Spagna also decorated a chapel in the fifteenth-century Church of Santa Maria delle Lagrime (St. Mary of the Tears) halfway between the town and the Trevi railroad station; an Adoration of the Magi in it is by Perugino.

↙ Rose of Umbria ↘

The young Clitunno and other streams and canals running nearly parallel to it cut across the plain below Trevi. The green valley becomes broader as the foothills recede and the Topino River, coming from the north, turns westward to join the waters flowing from other directions. The plain is vast enough to accommodate a regional air strip south of the city of Foligno.

Entering Foligno by car or on foot from its peripheral railroad station, the visitor notes plenty of cyclists, not a frequent sight in Umbria's many hill towns. Foligno, in fact, is one of the region's two major level cities; the other is Terni. With its more than 50,000 residents, Foligno is the third-largest population center of Umbria, and it keeps growing. It is an important traffic hub: A superhighway (National Route No. 75) links the Via Flaminia (National Route No. 3) with Assisi and Perugia; National Route No. 77 turns off the Flaminian Road to the small university town of Camerino and the city of Macerata in the neighboring Marche region. From Foligno railroad station a line branches off the Rome-Ancona route to Assisi, Perugia, and Terontola-Cortona (p. 28). Some trains coming from Rome proceed from Foligno to Assisi and the regional capital; travelers on trains bound for Ancona change in Foligno for Assisi and destinations beyond it.

My advice is to get off the national highways or to stop between trains and devote half a day, if not more, to exploring the city. The *folignati*, as its natives are called, are said to be more outgoing than are other Umbrians, "more open," as the standard phrase goes. Foligno sees a lot of commerce and transiting people; it's not only a road and rail pivot, but also a manufacturing city with many medium-sized and small industrial plants on its outskirts.

Apartments and houses for rent or purchase are easier to find in Foligno than in most other Umbrian centers. Various acquaintances of mine who wanted to move from Rome to some smaller provincial town settled here. "It's not the most stimulating and exciting place," one of the new residents told me, "but it is very quiet at night—such a relief after the noise in Rome until late. And if I want to go to some play or concert, I can be in Perugia in half an hour; Spoleto is the same short distance, and Assisi is even closer." Foligno, indeed, likes to be known as the "Rose of Umbria"—rose in the sense of the middle of a compass card.

This rose itself vaunts a remarkable center, the Piazza della Repubblica. This is one of the grand urban spaces of Umbria. On the east side is the so-called minor facade of the cathedral, providing access to the left transept of the twelfth-century edifice. With its three rose windows, elaborate Gothic double windows, and ornamentation inspired by classical Roman models, this side front is more impressive than is the principal facade of the church on the small Piazza del Duomo around the corner from the main square.

The interior of the large structure was remodeled in the Baroque mode in 1772 by the architect Giuseppe Piermarini; he was a native of Foligno who also built the elegant La Scala Opera House in Milan and other important projects in and near that city. Piermarini is not responsible for the triumphalist canopy above the main altar of the Foligno Cathedral, a faithful scale copy of Gian Lorenzo Bernini's baldachin over the papal altar in St. Peter's in Rome, executed toward the end of the seventeenth century. Only, Bernini's showy work in St. Peter's is of bronze, whereas the Foligno canopy with its spiral columns is of polished and gilt wood.

A large, gilt silver statue of St. Felician, patron saint of Foligno, that stood in a niche of the apse was vandalized one night in 1982 by thieves who wrenched off the most precious parts of the sculpture. Thefts in churches are a continuing grave problem in

Umbria as they are in other parts of Italy; looters who are experts in coping with locks, burglar alarms, and other security devices often act on commission from art traffickers. Yet whoever broke into the Foligno Cathedral wasn't interested in the artistic value of the saint's statue from the year 1700 (which was questionable anyway), but in the precious metal. St. Felician was bishop of Foligno in the second or third century, and is, among other things, credited with having consecrated St. Valentine of Terni (p. 86). Foligno celebrates the feast day of St. Felician on January 24 with a religious procession in the medieval city core.

A graceful arched passage spanning a side street joins the cathedral with the massive Palazzo Trinci on the northwest side of the main square. This three-story building with nineteenth-century brick columns and other neoclassical style elements added to its facade goes back to the Middle Ages. It was the residence of the powerful Trinci family, which claimed descent from the Lombards, and from 1305 to 1439 ruled Foligno. Their palace later became the seat of the papal government of the city and its territory; heavily damaged by Allied air raids during World War II, it has long been repaired.

Today the Palazzo Trinci contains a library, a small archeological museum with, mainly, Roman antiquities, several frescoed halls and corridors, and a picture gallery. This collection is a showcase of the so-called School of Foligno, a local art movement of the fifteenth century that was inspired by Benozzo Gozzoli in nearby Montefalco (p. 176). Its main representatives were Niccolò Liberatore, called L'Alunno (the disciple) and his son Lattanzio di Niccolò; their Madonnas, saints, archangels, and other religious figures display dramatic and somewhat stereotyped expressions, anticipating the mannerism of later Baroque art. The chapel of the palace was frescoed with a History of the Virgin cycle by Ottavio Nelli of Gubbio (p. 168) in 1424.

Don't expect to find the original of Raphael's Madonna of Foligno, one of his most renowned works, in the Palazzo Trinci or anywhere else in the city. It is today one of the chief treasures of the Vatican Picture Gallery. Napoleon had carried it off to Paris, but it was later returned to Italy with other plunder. The famous painting was commissioned by the wealthy Foligno humanist Sigismondo Conti—who after the latinizing fashion of the Renaissance called himself Sigismondo de Comitibus—as a votive offering in gratitude for being spared when his house was hit by lightning (or an artillery shell?). Raphael executed the panel (later transferred to a canvas) in 1511–12. Sigismondo is shown kneeling, being presented by St. Jerome to the Madonna, who is floating above the green hills of Umbria. St. Francis and St. John Baptist flank Sigismondo. There is a rainbow and the orange arc of what may be a thunderbolt or the trajectory of a missile that besiegers lobbed into Foligno in one of the factional wars that lacerated Umbria at that epoch. The impact on Sigismondo's tall house is visible; behind it are other houses and a tower. A copy of Raphael's masterpiece is above an altar in the left transept of the cathedral.

Diagonally opposite the cathedral's side facade, in the southwest of the main square, is City Hall, a structure from the thirteenth century that in the seventeenth century was rebuilt with a pompous row of six columns over a front portico. The building was surmounted by a battlemented Renaissance watchtower, which a 1997 earth shock toppled.

My favorite among Foligno's many examples of ancient architecture is Santa Maria Infraportas (the last word is Latin for "below the gates"). The squat Romanesque church with a porch and a massive, square bell tower, in the Piazza San Domenico on the western outskirts, goes back to the eleventh or twelfth century; different layers of bricks and stones are visible everywhere in the building. A chapel opening from the left nave is much older than the bulk of the edifice, possibly erected in early Christian times. It contains badly damaged frescoes that, according to experts, betray Byzantine influences. Masters of the Foligno School of Painting frescoed the naves and apse of the church with votive pictures and other devotional images. Among these artists were Pierantonio Mezzastris (1430–1506), an assistant and associate of Benozzo Gozzoli, who is also represented with many works in the Palazzo Trinci and various other churches in the district.

The town gates, to which the ancient church's name refers, have all disappeared, except one, the Porta Romana, now free-standing on the Via Umberto I, which is the shortest connection between the railroad station and the main square. Foligno's principal shopping street, lined with stores, banks, and old palaces, is the Corso Cavour, running from the square around the former Roman Gate near the rail station to the center. In the public park at the beginning of the corso is a monument of Niccolò Liberatore, L'Alunno (p. 129), who is regarded as the founder of the Foligno School of Painting.

The Topino, Umbria's third most important river next to the Tiber and the Nera, skirts Foligno's north between high walls that show their age. The river was diverted to its present bed in the thirteenth century; it used to flow where now the narrow Mill Canal cuts through the city's northern neighborhoods. Remains of an ancient Roman bridge ("Caesar's Bridge," local people say) can be seen there. Tanners and artisans plied their trades along the river's old course; robust arcades of their medieval workshops along the Mill Canal have survived.

The colorful Foligno Festival, revived after World War II to attract tourists, has very old roots. It is still known as the Giostra della Quintana, or Joust of the Quintain, and is a competition in which horsemen representing the city's ten ancient sections show off their speed and dexterity. The quintain was the fifth street in a Roman army camp; in it the legionnaires held exercises, bought merchandise from local tradesmen who had been admitted, and did their drinking. The joust, instead, is a medieval chivalrous tradition that lived on long in Italian towns.

In Foligno, between the twelfth and eighteenth centuries, the ten neighborhoods into which the city was divided staged a riding competition almost every year. The quintain or quintana had by then become personified in a wooden statue, supposed to embody Mars, the Roman god of war. The winner of the joust was the horseman who first hit the statue in its face with his lance, or toppled it.

In addition to the ten selected riders some 500 men, women, and children, all in gorgeous seventeenth-century costumes, act for the city government and the ten neighborhoods. They parade in the central streets and in the main square where the bishop of Foligno blesses the riders and their horses in the evening before the first of the joust's three rounds.

↙ *A Spellbinding Place* ↘

New York friends of mine who had taken a house near Siena for a month in spring wanted to explore Umbria, which isn't far away. They rented a car and dutifully visited Assisi, but found it touristy (they probably arrived there in the late morning when the town usually is crowded with visitors). Then Janet and her husband, Harvey, drove on for a few miles to have a look at the neighboring hill town, Spello. They fell at once in love with it, and stayed three days before returning to their rented house in Tuscany. When they told me afterward they were convinced they had hit on the essence of Umbria, I said, "It's one of my favorite places in that region too."

The approaches to Spello are solemn. A few hundred yards east of the Foligno-Perugia superhighway (National Route No. 75) and railroad line are the ruins of a Roman amphitheater. It was built in the plain with reddish stone blocks from Mt. Subasio, which dominates Assisi, in the first century A.D. The oval arena, 354 feet by 269 feet, with two entrances, must have had excellent acoustics, although it wasn't built for theatrical performances; even now, with the substructures worn away by looters and the passage of time, words said in a low voice at one end can be heard at the other. Today, pine trees and shrubbery are all around.

Behind the decayed amphitheater the town of Spello theatrically rises on a low spur of Mt. Subasio, surrounded by olive groves. Olive trees also bizarrely crown the flat top of the tall, square clock tower from the Middle Ages at the left side of the severe Consular Gate. This massive doorway is probably from Rome's Republican era, maybe the second century B.C. The structure is partly buried because the soil level has risen by six feet since it was erected, as earth and debris kept accumulating at its base through the centuries. One enters the town by the middle archway; the two former side entrances, of which only the upper parts are visible, are walled up. On the gate's reddish-yellow outer walls, above the central opening, are the life-size marble statues of a matron and two togaed men, apparently taken from Roman tombs near the town at an unspecified time.

Instead of proceeding at once into Spello's core, the visitor will do well to inspect the redoubtable fortifications to the left of the Consular Gate. These town walls were started by the Umbrians, and elaborately strengthened by the ancient Romans with walkways, battlements, watchtowers, billets for the garrison, storerooms, and aqueducts. During the Middle Ages the town's defenses were repeatedly razed and rebuilt; what has survived to this day still looks formidable.

Most impressive is the Porta Venere (Venus Gate), at some distance to the left of the Consular Gate, and visible also from the railroad trains and the superhighway. Built under Emperor Augustus, and most recently restored after World War II, it is a structure with three arched entrances between two tall, twelve-sided towers. The gate owes its name to a temple of Venus that once stood outside the town walls.

Spello was an Umbrian settlement of some importance, and a thriving center under the Romans, who called it Hispellum. The town claims to be the birthplace of the poet Sextus Propertius (circa 50 B.C.–circa 16 B.C.) although Assisi, Bettona, and a dozen other Umbrian towns too consider him their native son. The few clues to the poet's origins that are to be found in his *Elegies* furnish a case for Spello, but also for the other claimants: "You ask me, Tullius. . . . what is my lineage and where my home is," Propertius says in I/22. "I was begotten there where Umbria's hills border the rich and fruitfull plain below." Spello, at any rate, calls the polygonal towers flanking the Venus Gate the Towers of Propertius, and the street leading from the gate up into the town center the Via delle Torri di Properzio (Street of the Towers of Propertius).

To penetrate into Spello proper, take the Via Consolare from the Consular Gate. It curves up between weather-gray stone houses from the fourteenth and fifteenth centuries, and becomes the long, rising Via Cavour. On the left, halfway up, is the former Chapel of St. Anna or Tega Chapel (Cappella Tega), with patches of medieval frescoes that can be viewed, when the entrance is closed, through large plate-glass windows from the street.

On the right side of the elongated Piazza Matteotti, which bisects the Via Cavour, is the thirteenth-century Church of Santa Maria Maggiore, with a stout Romanesque bell tower topped by a four-sided stone pyramid. Inside, note the holy-water basin at the right near the entrance; it is a hollowed-out ancient Roman tombstone with bas-reliefs. The holy-water basin at the left is the adapted top part of an ancient column.

The so-called Baglioni Chapel farther to the left was frescoed by Pinturicchio, who had been commissioned by Troilo Baglioni, then prior of the church (he would later become bishop of Perugia). Pinturicchio executed the order between 1500 and 1503, painting an Annunciation, an Adoration, a Jesus Teaching at the Temple, and, on the ceiling, four Sibyls. The Annunciation includes the master's self-portrait with his signature, "Bernardinus Pinturicius Perusinus"; his patron, Troilo Baglioni, is pictured among the sages in the temple. Pinturicchio also painted a Madonna and Child in the sacristy. In 1521 the aged Perugino contributed a Pietà with Saints and a Madonna with Child on the left and right pillars at the entrance to the choir.

A new Civic Museum takes up eight rooms on the second floor of the building on the left of Santa Maria Maggiore. Its prize exhibit is a wooden Madonna and Child sculpture from the early thirteenth century whose original polychrome paint was recently restored. The severe Gothic work, stressing vertical lines and a rigid posture, is by an unidentified master from Spello or Spoleto. The collection also contains detached frescoes from various churches in the town and in its surroundings, old paintings by local artists who were influenced by Perugino and Pinturicchio, church vestments, and a big, exuberant reliquary in silver and lapis lazuli, dated 1788. Look out of the museum's windows, and you see orderly rows of olive trees on a slope.

A little higher up, also on the right side of the street, is the fourteenth-century Church of Sant'Andrea. In its right transept is a large Madonna with Four Saints by Pinturicchio (1508), then assisted by Eusebio da San Giorgio, who was also a disciple of Perugino. Curiously, Pinturicchio painted near one of the saints a pulpit with two sheets of paper on which he transcribed an actual letter he had received from Gentile Baglioni, Bishop of Orvieto, regarding an offer of work received from Siena. Did the artist want to show how much he was in demand?

Still higher up is the rectangular main square, Piazza della Repubblica, with a sixteenth-century fountain and a towered Town Hall, a mostly modern building that incorporates some medieval structures. Past another old church, San Lorenzo, the visitor reaches the loftiest point of Spello, the belvedere, with a panorama of the green Topino Valley, the oval ruins of the amphitheater, the rail tracks and highways in the foreground, and the hills of Montefalco, Assisi, and Perugia on the horizon. The belvedere is crowned with the remaining walls of one of the fortresses that Cardinal Albornoz had built in the region.

Strolling around the picture-book town with its narrow, sloping streets, hidden corners, and many archways on a weekday morning, one wouldn't believe it counts 8,000 inhabitants—so few people are to be seen. Many have left early in the morning for jobs or classes in Foligno, Assisi, or Perugia. The commuters will be back in the late afternoon when the dreamy town awakens.

The feast of Corpus Christi (p. 11) brings unusual crowds to Spello to admire the gaudy displays of the Infiorata (flower festival). Some central streets of Spello are for that day carpeted with flowers of different colors, arranged in artistic patterns on the model of the much older Infiorata of Genzano di Roma, one of the towns in the hillside southeast of the Italian capital.

The tentacles of the international tourist industry now reach also into this quiet Umbrian town. Diagonally opposite the main church, Santa Maria Maggiore, is a new four-star hotel in a restructured palazzo that goes back to the fourteenth century. It offers, says its English-language folder, "soft classical comfort that hides the modern technologies with intelligence, so as not to spoil the atmosphere of other times."

My New York friends found the establishment too pretentious, and put up in a more modest place near the belvedere whose calm and panorama they loved. They took their main meals, however, at the restaurant Il Mulino, which is across the street from the fancy hotel, and under the same management. I too had lunch there, with other friends of mine, during a later visit, and we were impressed by the food and service, less by the ambiance. The vaulted dining room, with a newly built fireplace, had belonged to a fourteenth-century oil mill (an old millstone decorates the entrance); stone blocks from some Roman building that may be 2,000 years old are visible in a corridor; the waiters were in formal black-tie attire. It all looked like a movie set rather than the old, simple Spello I had first known decades earlier.

5

~·:·~

Saints and Silence

From Spello to Assisi it is just a few minutes by road or rail. The traveler who looks northeast from the superhighway or the reassuringly old-fashioned Assisi railroad station beholds the sublime little town stretching out almost languidly on a gentle spur of Mt. Subasio. The imposing church-and-monastery complex of St. Francis, incongruously resembling a high-bowed white ship about to sail northwestward, is on the left; the campanile of St. Clare's rises on the right; the medieval fortress on top of the hill looms above the church steeples, the brown roofs, the white and pink houses, and the green patches of many little gardens.

Before ascending to Assisi proper the visitor should pause in the hamlet between the rail station and the highway, almost 1,000 feet below the town, to see the humble site where the Franciscan movement was born and where its founder died.

What St. Francis started in the valley at the foot of his birth-place has in the nearly 800 years since then grown into a world-wide community of more than 30,000 friars (of whom 20,000 are priests) and many thousands of nuns in a family of religious orders. A metropolis in California and cities elsewhere are named after St. Francis; thousands of Roman Catholic laypeople in many countries belong to his Third Order; and many non-Catholics and non-Christians as well as secular pacifists and environmentalists sympathize with the Franciscan message of poverty, humility, peace, and love of nature and all its creatures.

Every year Catholics, adherents of other faiths, agnostics, and political leftists take part in a peace march—actually, a relaxed hike—over all or a part of the sixteen miles from Perugia to Assisi. Pope John Paul II in 1986 presided over an interfaith meeting in Assisi that was attended by representatives of various Christian denominations, Jews, Muslims, and Buddhist monks.

The visitor cannot miss Santa Maria degli Angeli (St. Mary of the Angels), the pilgrimage church that grandly shelters the poor cradle of Franciscanism. It stands a few steps south of the railroad tracks and a few hundred yards from the exit of the superhighway. The high-domed structure was built between 1569 and 1679, and it is believed that Iacopo Barozzi, known as Il Vignola, the chief architect of St. Peter's in Rome after Michelangelo, was involved in the project in an advisory capacity. An earthquake in 1832 caused heavy damages, subsequently repaired. A new facade was erected in 1928. To me the huge church in the Roman Baroque style appeared always bombastic; St. Francis would have been horrified.

Santa Maria degli Angeli is open from early morning to twelve noon and from two P.M. to nightfall daily. The vast dimensions of the church's stuccoed interior make the vestiges connected with St. Francis's life and death seem particularly small and meek.

Directly below the lofty cupola is the Portiuncula (in Italian, Porziuncola), meaning "little section," the saint's first house of prayer. The tiny, rectangular stone building was an abandoned and ruined chapel in a forest in 1210 when the twenty-eight-year-old Francis obtained its use from the Benedictines of Mt. Subasio who had owned it for centuries. The yearly rental was a bucket of fish from the Tescio, the stream skirting Assisi at its north.

The young ascetic and mystic had by then broken with his wealthy father, had formally renounced his inheritance, and was wearing a coarse cloak instead of the fashionable dress of his earlier years. His father, Pietro di Bernardone, was a cloth merchant belonging to the emergent, affluent middle class. Together with other tradesmen, and protected by armed guards hired in Assisi, he would journey to France on business every year.

From one of those travels he had brought home a young wife; she would be known in Assisi as Pica, possibly an abbreviation of Picardie, the northern French province of which she may have been a native. When Pietro di Bernardone on his return from a later journey found a baby boy who had been baptized Giovanni, he changed his son's name to Francesco. This sounded odd at the time, but was supposed to hint that the child was half French.

Assisi in the early thirteenth century enjoyed a measure of prosperity like other Umbrian towns, although they were often at war with one another or with enemies from outside the region. Assisi had a German garrison because the town belonged to the domains of Philip of Swabia; nearby Perugia was papal.

At the age of twenty Francesco fought against the Perugians with an Assisi force, was captured, and spent a year as a prisoner of war in Perugia. He would never like that city. Much later, gentle St. Francis in a fit of anger was to curse Perugia: "Your heart is puffed up with arrogance. . . . You pillage your neighbors and you kill many of them. And so I tell you, if you don't convert very soon, the Lord is preparing a terrible vengeance against you." The saint warned the Perugians they would suffer civil war, which would cause unending evils; his prophecy was to come all too true in the fourteenth and fifteenth centuries.

The conversion of Francesco—whom his Assisi boon companions once had crowned as "king of revelers"—occurred during another aborted military venture. He had joined the troops of a *condottiere* for fighting in Southern Italy but didn't get any farther with them than Spoleto, where he dropped out after an episode of sickness and spiritual crisis.

Soon St. Francis and his first disciples lived in the Portiuncula and in rudimentary cells they had built nearby, devoting themselves to poverty and work among the destitute. Pope Innocent III in 1210 approved the first rule that the small lay brotherhood had given itself.

It was in the Portiuncula also that St. Clare, then eighteen years old, had her hair shorn and was given a nun's habit by Francis. Born Chiara d'Offreduccio degli Scifi, the daughter of a rich count, the young woman had run away from their Assisi mansion with a girl relative on Palm Sunday of the year 1212 to become a follower of Friar Francis. The new nun first found shelter in convents in the vicinity of Assisi, and eventually founded the Order of the Poor Clares. St. Clare was to survive St. Francis by twenty-seven years.

Today the Portiuncula, dwarfed by the church above and around it, attracts uncounted pilgrims. There are always at least a few devotees praying in front of the little old chapel, and rows of votive candles flicker at all times. The facade of the Portiuncula, in bright limestone from Mt. Subasio, carries on its upper half an 1829 fresco by the German painter Johann Friedrich Overbeck, a precursor of the pre-Raphaelite fraternity; it represents St. Francis imploring indulgence from Jesus and the Virgin Mary. A little open turret in Gothic style above the gable is a modern addition containing a fifteenth-century statuette of the Virgin and Child. The outer and inner walls of the Portiuncula show traces of old frescoes that were long covered by thick layers of soot from the candles that had burned there for centuries. After the 1997–98 earth tremors, art restorers gingerly cleaned the walls of the Portiuncula and were cheered to find that the walls had suffered no damages and that there were no cracks.

Instead, under the soot and dust of the gable a triangular Crucifixion came to light. Experts suggested that the fresco may have been painted by Perugino when he was in Assisi in the summer of 1486. The long-admired altarpiece in the Portiuncula, an Annunciation, is the work of the priest-artist Ilario of Viterbo, circa 1393.

Behind the Portiuncula, at the right side of the choir, is the Chapel of the Transit with the cell in which St. Francis died—or "transited" to afterlife—on October 4, 1226. Two years earlier he had received the stigmata (marks on his hands, feet, and side resembling the wounds of the crucified Jesus). That mystical event had occurred after forty days of prayer and fasting in the monastery the saint had built at 3,701 feet above sea level on La Verna, a rocky mountain in Tuscany between the sources of the

Tiber and the Arno. Since then he had been plagued by various diseases, and eventually returned to the Portiuncula to await "Sister Death" (the word *morte*, death, has the feminine gender). St. Francis is said to have died on the bare floor, wrapped in a coat borrowed from the guardian.

The wooden door of the chapel-cell is from that time. The frescoes inside, showing Franciscan saints, are by Lo Spagna of Spoleto, and a terra-cotta statue of St. Francis in a niche is by Andrea della Robbia. A small cupboard holds Franciscan relics. East of the sacristy is a little garden with roses that are said to have grown without thorns ever since the days of St. Francis. The saint, according to legend, was one summer night tempted by the demon and, to do penance, threw himself into a bed of thorny roses. That episode is depicted in frescoes by Tiberio d'Assisi (1518) in the nearby Chapel of the Roses. Botanists have classified the thornless rose variety, which has reddish leaves, as *rosa canina asisiensis* (Assisi dog rose).

The Portiuncula and the church sheltering it suffered only slight damages during the earth tremors of 1997–98.

The anniversary of St. Francis's death, October 4, is solemnly observed in Assisi every year, and both the Church of Santa Maria degli Angeli and the Church of St. Francis are always on that day crowded with friars and other pilgrims. Cardinals and Italian government officials visit the Umbrian town to attend commemorative rites.

✨ *Blue-Jeans Friars* ✨

From the church and the unremarkable hamlet of Santa Maria degli Angeli one can walk up to Assisi in forty-five minutes or take the public bus, which runs at half-hour intervals. Motorists find four pay parking lots accommodating 700 cars and thirty-four tourist buses on the outskirts of the walled town, two of them close to the Basilica of St. Francis.

Visitors to Assisi at once notice the town's neatness, and in the evening—when most foreigners are gone—will be struck by its silence. The streets are among the cleanest in all of Italy, although throngs of tourists and pilgrims troop around in them every day in the year; sanitation personnel tirelessly clean up after them. The bright gray stones from Mt. Subasio, with which the old buildings were constructed, seem all freshly scrubbed. Little gardens on various levels are squeezed in between houses, and flowers are in many windows, brightening up the townscape. One of the delights of the medieval place is exploring its many side lanes with their stairways and walls overgrown with vegetation.

While the foreigners for whom the town is kept so tidy bring in a lot of money, Assisi's permanent population—24,000 at latest report—is diminishing. A local physician, Eduardo Minciotti, M.D., explained why: "The cost of living here is very high because tourism is by now the master of the town. Our local administrators have never managed to protect the residents, whose essential needs they don't even understand. . . . Assisi is increasingly becoming a town of hotel keepers and pizzeria owners. Other people are moving out."

The earthquake of September 1997 and the many aftershocks, which hit Assisi hard, caused huge problems for the citizenry and the local authorities. The tourist business fell off drastically for months, and Town Hall pleaded with the Region of Umbria in Perugia and the central government in Rome for help.

A woman at the post office told me in May 1998, "Assisi may

have been better off in the days of St. Francis when there were no tourists and no souvenir peddlers." In the early thirteenth century, about 22,000 people are estimated to have lived in Assisi, which for that epoch made it an important center; quite a few of its inhabitants were considered wealthy.

Strolling along the nearly parallel main streets that cross the town for almost a mile from the Porta Nuova (New Gate) at its southeast to the Basilica of St. Francis, northwest, the visitor notices that in addition to the hotels and pizza parlors, of which the good doctor spoke, there are also boutiques with designer clothes and leatherware, jewelry shops, emporiums offering Umbrian olive oil and truffles, fine restaurants, and real estate agencies.

Pottery, religious kitsch, and T-shirts with Assisi views are displayed next to bottles with a murky "San Francesco Liquor," purporting to have been distilled from black truffles and walnuts. St. Francis may have drunk a little of the local wine now and then, but surely no hard stuff. Some of the souvenir shops and eating places are on the street level of stately Renaissance palazzi and are known to pay stiff rents.

Lady Poverty, whom St. Francis wooed, does not appear to inhabit present-day Assisi. True, the friars and nuns in the town still wear the Franciscan habit, the three knots in their rope girdle signifying poverty, chastity, and obedience. On the latest of many visits to Assisi, however, I saw a young monk, his blue jeans peeking out from under his coarse brown cowl; at least he wore not Gucci loafers but sandals. I mused about how a contemporary St. Francis would have to dress to distinguish himself from the young Umbrian fellows in stone-washed and artfully tattered designer jeans who climb into their Porsches and Ferraris.

Devotees of St. Francis will at once visit the basilica named after him, which actually comprises two churches, one above the other, with a crypt underneath. It is one of the oldest Gothic religious buildings in Italy. Friar Elias, a close friend of the saint who for some years after his death served as the Franciscan Order's general superior, is credited with having conceived the idea of a double church and adjacent monastery, and of having commissioned and supervised the architects.

As a site for the construction project, a wealthy Assisi citizen donated a large plot of land on a spur of Mt. Subasio, popularly known as Infernal Hill because evildoers had been executed on it. Admirers of St. Francis all over Europe contributed money. The greatest painters of the epoch, Cimabue and Giotto, were to fresco the edifice.

The learned Pope Gregory IX personally laid the cornerstone the day after he had solemnly canonized St. Francis in July 1228, less than two years after the saint's death. Pope Innocent IV consecrated the still unfinished twin church in 1253.

The grand medieval edifice on the whole weathered the many earth shocks that rocked Umbria through the centuries—until the 1997 quake. The initial tremors damaged above all the Upper Church and its art works, forcing the restorers to close that part of the building to the public for an indefinite (and surely lengthy) period. From outside, visitors may glimpse architectural details behind the scaffolding.

The facade of the complex is that of the Upper Church, looking eastward onto the large Upper Square of St. Francis and toward the town center. The symbols of the four Evangelists in relief are beneath a magnificently elaborate rose window. A Loggia of Benedictions in the Renaissance style was added at the left of the facade in the early seventeenth century to provide an outdoor pulpit from which the clergy could address pilgrims in the piazza.

The Lower Church, which one enters through its south door from the Lower Square of St. Francis, is gloomy and even on the hottest summer day may feel chilly. Its side chapels shelter the tombs of medieval noble personages. The abundant murals in the chapels, in the apse, and on the low ceiling vaults are by Cimabue and his followers, by pupils of Giotto (probably after designs by the master himself), and by other painters of their day. A powerful fresco, Madonna with Child, Four Angels, and St. Francis, on the vault of the right transept is generally attributed to Cimabue.

Four triangular spaces behind the main altar are frescoed with allegories of Poverty, Chastity, and Obedience, and with an Apotheosis of St. Francis, executed by disciples of Giotto following his instructions. The triangle facing the altar and closest to the nave, possibly by Giotto himself, represents St. Francis being married by Jesus to Lady Poverty, who wears rags and a crown of thorns; Ladies Chastity and Obedience are in attendance.

A small chapel in the rear of the Lower Church, opposite the entrance, leads through a door in its left wall to a beautiful two-storied cloister with tall cypresses, once the friars' cemetery.

Double stairs halfway from the nave of the Lower Church, their steps worn smooth by the shoes of uncounted pilgrims, descend to the crypt. This vaulted basement chapel was rebuilt in 1818 after the remains of St. Francis had been located at the end of a long search; they were discovered in a stone coffin under three travertine slabs. Followers of St. Francis had hidden the coffin long ago for fear that rivals of Assisi, maybe the detested

Perugians, might steal it. Relic-snatching was common in centuries past, and not only in Umbria.

Now the rough coffin is visible, resting on a stone pedestal behind the crypt's altar. Fresh flowers and burning candles abound at all times.

⌣∴ *Famous Frescoes* ∵∾

Before the 1997 earthquake the Upper Church could be reached by narrow stairs from a small corridor off the left transept of the Lower Church or, more conveniently, over a double open-air staircase linking the two levels of the Square of St. Francis. In contrast to the somber lower part of the double basilica, the Upper Church, receiving light through tall stained-glass windows, used to be luminous.

In the earthquake of September 26, 1997, portions of the frescoed ceiling, together measuring 360 square feet, of the high-vaulted Upper Church collapsed. Next day, four persons—two art officials from Perugia and two Franciscan friars—who were inspecting the damages were killed by falling debris during a strong aftershock. Frescoes depicting St. Jerome, attributed to the young Giotto or his assistants, and St. Matthew, believed to be a work of Cimabue, as well as sections representing the starred sky, were among the destroyed parts of the ceiling. Restorers at once started collecting and painstakingly sifting tens of thousands of ceiling fragments—some as tiny as rice seeds—in an effort to piece together such parts of the frescoes as could be saved. The salvage project is expected to take years.

The celebrated Giotto frescoes on the two sides of the Upper

Church's nave, which were ailing already long before the 1997–98 tremors, escaped major harm, but they were declared off limits to visitors and protected by special scaffolding for lengthy tests and restoration work. Visitors to Assisi will for considerable time have to content themselves with reproductions of the historic Giotto cycle.

Art historians keep debating which panels are by Giotto himself and which were painted, probably under his supervision, by disciples from Tuscany. Artists from Rome took a hand in decorating the Upper Church too.

In the 1980s conservationists obtained from the Italian Air Force the cessation of any further exercises in the air space in a wide radius above Assisi because the sonic booms might cause the murals to crack or flake.

The pictures by Giotto and his assistants take up the lower of two rows of panels on either side of the nave. They form a cycle of twenty-eight frescoes illustrating the life, death, and afterlife of St. Francis. (The four last paintings are attributed to the fourteenth-century Tuscan artist identified as the Master of St. Cecilia, after a picture in the Uffizi Gallery in Florence.)

The epochal importance of the Assisi frescoes lies in the fact that they mark the transition from the two-dimensional rigidy of Byzantine art to Renaissance painting with depth, movement, and eventually, perspective. Giotto here heralded western art.

Among the most famous of the Giotto frescoes are No. 2, showing the saint giving his coat to a poor man with medieval Assisi as background; No. 5, St. Francis returning his showy clothes to his irate father while the bishop of Assisi covers him with a cloak; No. 8, the saint appearing to his brethren in a fiery chariot; No. 10, St. Francis expelling demons from Arezzo; No.

12, the saint in ecstasis, with four stunned friars; No. 13, St. Francis building a crèche (a Nativity scene); No. 15, his sermon to the birds, with sparrows, quail, pigeons, and other species well rendered; No. 19, the saint receiving the stigmata; No. 20, death and funeral of St. Francis; No. 23, grieving nuns of St. Clare.

The Giotto frescoes draw on the jumble of factual episodes, anecdotes, and legends that originated already during the lifetime of St. Francis, proliferated after his death, and would eventually be collected in the *Fioretti* (*Little Flowers*). The oldest known manuscript containing those stories is from A.D. 1390; the first printed version was published at Vicenza in 1476. Because of their sturdy language, their flashes of humor, and their occasional earthiness (like that of the early Tuscan novels), the *Fioretti* of St. Francis are a monument of Italian literature that has been called a folk masterpiece. There is precious little theology in those stories, but plenty of characterization and concrete, lively detail.

St. Francis, incidentally, wrote poetry himself. Only one canticle by him has come to us, and it is among the first poems written in the Italian vernacular instead of in Latin or Provençal. This *Canticle to Brother Sun* praises the Lord "for all your creatures." In his reverence for nature, as expressed in his poem, St. Francis appears as an early forerunner of Rousseau, the nineteenth-century Romantics, Thoreau, and the present-day ecological movement.

As for the Giotto frescoes, it would be irreverent to call them a sacred comic strip. Yet during earlier visits I have overheard more than one sightseer audibly whisper (in the belief to be making a witty remark never uttered before): "What a pity the balloons with the dialogue are missing."

The upper row of frescoes, interrupted by the stained-glass windows, are biblical scenes by the Roman fourteenth-century painter Pietro Cavallini and by assistants and pupils of Cimabue. That thirteenth-century master and presumed teacher of Giotto is believed to have personally painted a dramatic Crucifixion in the left transept; oxidation of the lead in the colors used by Cimabue (if he really was the artist) unfortunately caused the masterpiece to darken so that it looks today like the negative of a photo. Followers of Cimabue frescoed the transepts and choir with scenes from the Book of Revelation, the life and death of the Virgin, angels, apostles, evangelists, and saints.

Groups of tourists would stop at each panel of the Giotto frescoes and at the other works of art while a guide explained their meaning and history; many visitors, however, would just walk around the Upper and Lower Church and descend to the crypt, all in a quarter of an hour. Yet others come to pray.

To be admitted to the Franciscan Convent adjoining the twin basilica, visitors must be guided by a friar, who will be found in the sacristy of the Lower Church. They will be shown the grand, two-storied cloister and various frescoed halls. A money contribution is expected; cash gifts for the upkeep of the buildings and for Franciscan activities are also solicited by signs on little desks, manned by friars.

Pope John Paul II prayed before the tomb of St. Francis soon after the earthquake during a tour of areas in the Umbria and Marches regions that had suffered the worst damages.

The Basilica of St. Francis today—behind its braces, trusses, ladders, and cranes—remains a unique complex. Turn around, and view Assisi.

From the Upper Square of St. Francis one walks across a lawn to the slightly inclined, 600-yard-long Via di San Francesco toward the center of town. At the end of it, the short and narrow

Via Portica leads to the interesting main square, the Piazza del Comune.

On the north side of the Via Portica is the entrance to the Archeological Museum and to the remains of the Roman Forum. That commercial and administrative center of what was the flourishing Roman city of Asisium extended eight feet below the level of the present main square. Patches of the ancient pavement, walls with Latin inscriptions, and various stone markers can be seen. The museum contains Etruscan and Roman material.

The square above the Roman Forum is dominated by the tall, battlemented Civic Tower from the thirteenth century on its north side. To its left is the fourteenth-century Palace of the People's Captain, the commander of the militia. Right of the tower is the well-preserved portico of a Temple of Minerva, with six elegant Corinthian columns of travertine. The interior of the shrine honoring the ancient goddess of learning and handicrafts was in the sixteenth century transformed into a church dedicated to the cult of the Virgin Mary.

Catercornered opposite, at the piazza's south side, is the fourteenth-century Town Hall; a fountain with steps is in front of it. The Municipal Picture Gallery (Pinacoteca) occupies parts of a building on the right side of the Town Hall. The small collection contains frescoes detached from various local churches and palaces, a damaged Madonna in Majesty by a follower of Giotto, and a St. Francis Blessing Assisi by the Orvieto painter Cesare Sermei (1584–1668).

The cathedral, dedicated to St. Rufinus, the martyred first bishop of Assisi (fourth century), is a short walk east of the main square. It is a Romanesque-Gothic edifice with a massive, square bell tower dating from the tenth century and later rebuilt and expanded. The facade, with rose windows over each of the three entrances, geometric decorations, and symbolic reliefs, is one of the most beautiful church fronts in all of Umbria.

In the right nave, close to the portal, is the ancient font where St. Francis and St. Clare were presumably baptized. Another newborn child, christened there twelve years after St. Francis, was a Swabian prince who would be brought up in Sicily among Saracens and was to become the mighty Emperor Frederick II, the *stupor mundi* (amazement of the world) of his stormy times.

↙ St. Clare's Assisi ↘

On the northeastern outskirts of the town are the remains of a Roman amphitheater, now with a few houses and gardens inside its ruined elliptical walls. During the twelfth century bull runs were still held in that ancient arena.

The church over the tomb of St. Clare is in the southeast corner of Assisi, an architectural and urban counterpoint to the Basilica and Convent of St. Francis across town. Built in layers of pink and bright gray stones between 1257 and 1265, St. Clare's is supported on its north side by two sturdy arched buttresses; the simple facade is graced by an intricate rose window. From the steps leading up to the portal and from the parapet of the square in front of it a grand panorama of the town, the hillside, and the charming valley can be enjoyed.

The inside of the church is austere, focusing on a huge, painted crucifix in the apse, which recalls Byzantine models; it is the work of an unidentified late-thirteenth-century artist whom the experts call the Master of Santa Chiara (St. Clare's). He is believed to have executed also a painting representing St. Clare and episodes of her life in the right transept. A Death and Funeral of St. Clare nearby is by a frescoist of the Giotto school. Two stairs descend from the nave to the crypt, which was built in the nineteenth century. The coffin with St. Clare's remains is under its main altar.

The Fortress, or Rocca Maggiore, is an oblong gray ruin sitting on the softly rounded top of the hill, some 400 feet above the lower neighborhoods of Assisi. Reachable by the curving Via della Rocca from the cathedral and the amphitheater, the medieval stronghold can be visited, and is noteworthy for its military architecture and, above all, for the sweeping views of the town and the Umbrian countryside. A bookshop offers literature about the fortress and Assisi as well as picture postcards. There is also a small Museum of Martyrdom and Torture, which may appeal to the lovers of the grisly.

Reading up on the history of the ruin, the visitor realizes that it is the enduring symbol of the wars, feuds between cities and between aristocratic clans, and frequent violence that were the grim Umbrian reality at the time of St. Francis's and St. Clare's mysticism as well as during the following centuries. Emperor Frederick Barbarossa had a castle erected on the hill above Assisi to tighten his grip on this part of the region. His grandson, baptized Frederick Roger in the Cathedral of Assisi (p. 154), was born at Iesi in the neighboring Marche region in 1194, lived as an infant in the hilltop stronghold, at the age of three was crowned King of Sicily in Palermo, later won also the title King of Germany, and in 1220 was crowned Holy Roman Emperor as Frederick II in Rome. Theoretically, St. Francis and St. Clare were his subjects.

However, the people of Assisi had destroyed the fortress that scowled on their town in an uprising in 1198. The emperor would eventually get even with the rebellious town. In the fourteenth century the unsentimental Cardinal Albornoz didn't bypass the birthplace of St. Francis in his strategic design for Umbria, and had the castle above Assisi rebuilt on a grander scale than before.

For hundreds of years the fortress saw sieges, sorties, intrigues—at one time it was given as a dowry to Lucrezia Borgia by her father, Pope Alexander VI—and crimes. The Rocca Maggiore interlocks with the walls that envelop the town; an outwork in the northeast corner of Assisi's fortifications is called the Rocca Minore.

Admirers of St. Francis and St. Clare will walk from Assisi's Porta Nuova, the gate at the southeast end of the walled town, to the little church and nunnery of San Damiano, half a mile downhill. The convent, among olive groves and cypresses, was founded by St. Francis; after 1212 it sheltered St. Clare and her first followers, and in 1253 St. Clare died in it.

The modest stone building looks like a farmhouse, to which a low porch has been added. From a square window halfway up the rough facade St. Clare is said to have put to flight Muslim soldiery at the service of Emperor Frederick in 1241 by holding up a monstrance and thereby frightening them. Maybe the glittering receptacle containing the consecrated host seemed to the marauders a mysterious and magic weapon. Frederick, who spoke Arabic (and five other languages), had Islamic soldiers among his military forces and had no compunction about using them in his continual struggle with the papacy. He had sent a detachment to Assisi to punish the town, long an imperial possession, for siding with the papal party—treason in Frederick's eyes.

Visitors to the nunnery will be shown the poor refectory where

St. Clare and her companions had their meals; the so-called garden of St. Clare, a narrow terrace with a view of the plain; and the spot where the saint died. St. Clare was proclaimed the universal patroness of television by Pope Pius XII in 1957 because of her visions and also because of her mother's supposed prophecy that she would become "a light to illumine the world."

Another rewarding side trip is to the Hermitage of the Prisons (Eremo delle Carceri), a once-lonely place in an oak forest at 2,595 feet above sea level, two miles east of Assisi, where St. Francis loved to retire for prayer and meditation. In the fifteenth century St. Bernardine of Siena, a Franciscan (p. 47), built a small convent there, which because of its narrow cells, small windows, and perilous location above a ravine was likened to a prison by local people. The name stuck.

The hermitage can be reached from Assisi on foot over a narrow road in little more than an hour, or by car in fifteen minutes. A friar will point out the tiny cave where St. Francis used to sleep on a bed of rocks, and a lower one where he prayed. It is through a cleft in a nearby rock that, according to legend, Satan escaped after tempting the saint in vain. An old ilex is known as the "bird tree" because St. Francis is said to have conducted mystical dialogues with the birds that used to gather on it. (His sermon to the birds, as depicted by Giotto, instead was delivered near Bevagna, p. 180)

From the "prisons" a path leads up to the top of Mt. Subasio, requiring strenuous walking for seventy to ninety minutes. At 4,232 feet altitude the summit commands a vast panorama of Apennine peaks and ranges and of Lake Trasimeno to the west.

The flowers that bloom on the broad meadows of Mt. Subasio early in the warm season are conspicuous in Assisi's Calendimaggio (May Day) festivities, now held on the first Thursday in May. Posies are put on the windows of nubile girls, and Madonna Primavera (Lady Spring), personified by a pretty young woman, holds a bouquet as she is receiving tributes. Music bands and other groups in medieval costumes, representing the lower and upper neighborhoods of the town—often violently feuding in past centuries—jointly parade in the main square.

The spring festival, going back to antiquity, draws visitors from all over Umbria and many tourists to Assisi. The young Francis, before becoming a saint, was presumably among the Calendimaggio revelers.

6

Three Umbrian Gems

My three favorite towns in the region are Gubbio, Montefalco, and Todi.

To drive from Perugia to Gubbio takes less than an hour, a most pleasant trip up and down undramatic hills green with olive trees, and over an easy pass rising to 2,172 feet above sea level. At the frequent bends the driver will have to slow down because the highway is narrow, though well maintained. Several points afford panoramas of soothing Umbrian views.

Starting from Ponte San Giovanni, the industrial suburb of the regional capital, the traveler crosses the Tiber and proceeds on Superhighway E-75 for a couple of miles to the exit for the hamlet of Bosco. The word means forest, and the place is believed to have once been a sacred grove dedicated to Bacchus, the god of wine; today it is a commuters' neighborhood of Perugia. Take National Route No. 298, the old Via Eugubina. The name is derived from Iguvium, as the town that today is Gubbio was in antiquity called by Umbrians and Romans. Natives of it like to be known as *eugubini*.

Often I don't drive to Gubbio right away because I first want to visit with friends who live on a farm in the countryside near the town. After a long stretch on the Via Eugubina without any houses, I turn off at the hamlet of Scritto to take a so-called "white road," which means an unpaved track covered with sand and pebbles. On a nearby hill stands a ruined medieval castle, Vallingegno, looking into the valley of the Cascio, the stream that joins the Tiber near Torgiano. The castle belonged to various lordly clans through the centuries. St. Francis of Assisi is believed to have stayed in it—or maybe in a nearby old abbey—for some time; there are few places in Umbria that don't claim the saint lived, preached, or spent the night there once.

At a point known as Pratale, meaning "a stretch of grassland," I park the car at the side of the narrow "white road" as well as I can, and walk down a steep path strewn with small rocks and pebbles to the farm. My friends don't expect me, but they are used to unannounced visitors. There is no way of getting in touch with them beforehand except by mail or telegram. They have no telephone and don't want one; they have no television either, but the children at times invite themselves to the house of a distant neighbor to watch some program.

In 1980 Etain, who is British, and her Swiss companion, Martin, bought the small hill farm, have run it ever since, and have in it brought up their three children, Melissa, Ben, and

Camilla. The kids didn't have to go to school, which is five miles distant, because their mother satisfied the local authorities that she was capable of teaching them at home. Etain's educational efforts were successful; Melissa, the oldest of the trio, passed the high school graduation exams for expatriate students at the British consulate in Rome, and went on to London University. While I am writing this the two younger children are still studying with their mother every day during the school year.

The farm has twenty-five acres of pasture and woodland, an olive grove, many fruit trees, and two vegetable patches. Etain and Martin keep a small herd of Sardinian milk sheep as well as chickens, ducks, rabbits, and donkeys. They eat the vegetables and fruits they grow, the eggs the hens lay, and the cheese and yogurt they make, and for cooking use the "extra-virgin" product pressed in a nearby oil mill from their own olives. Money for other food they need and for diverse expenses is earned by selling surplus produce and by taking in paying guests, some of whom love to lend a hand for farmwork.

In April 1984 a major earthquake wrecked the old stone farmhouse, but nobody was hurt. Like other owners of damaged property in the stricken area, Etain and Martin were promised rehabilitation subsidies from the Regional Government, but actual payments came only in hesitant installments. Somehow, between 1985 and 1988, the expatriate family rebuilt their home with recycled wood—mostly discarded railway sleepers—and with stone that abounds in the neighborhood. The new house, around a central courtyard, is now in the shape of an ancient Roman villa. Many former guests and other volunteers came with sleeping bags to help in the reconstruction work.

I like the new place with its vast common room and kitchen,

several bedrooms that are really just cabins with mattresses, a library stacked mostly with paperbacks left behind by guests, a bathhouse, and a workshop. I have met a variety of guests at Etain and Martin's—Americans, Australians, world travelers of various nationalities who would tramp on after a little stay, and Italians fascinated by what they call *agroturismo*, meaning holidays on the farm. Melissa, Ben, and Camilla, though not going to school, had plenty of chances for socializing.

Agroturismo has lately spread in Italy, particularly in Tuscany and Umbria. Etain and Martin were among the first hosts. Now quite a few foreigners own *casolari* (farmhouses) in the comparatively thinly populated land between Perugia and Gubbio, as well as in other districts of Umbria. Almost all of them have fixed up their properties, even rebuilt or restructured the old houses; some like the Pratale couple shelter paying guests, and others who don't but have an extra room or space for a spare bed or sleeping bag often have a waiting list of would-be nonpaying visitors.

Although Etain, Martin, and their children are to some extent leading a self-contained life, they are not cut off from the outside world. They visit Gubbio and Perugia from time to time. In winter, however, when paying guests are rare and the many cats and farm animals of Pratale may be the only company besides the family members, it must be lonely at home. Before Melissa left for London she used to talk about Gubbio as if it were a big, lively city; the younger children still do.

ᝆ: Stern Gubbio :ᝍ

Actually, Gubbio is a rather isolated and very quiet town of 31,000 inhabitants with an old center that climbs the steep slope of Mt. Ingino, and with modern suburbs spreading in a broad plain at its foot. A railroad that linked Gubbio eastward with Fossato di Vico on the Rome-Ancona line and with Umbértide and Perugia on the Central Umbrian Railway to its west was destroyed during World War II and has never been reactivated. Some of the sleepers of its tracks went into Etain and Martin's rebuilt farmhouse.

The historic core of Gubbio—essentially five parallel streets, each on a different level—looks stern, if not grim. The gray stones of the medieval houses have darkened over the centuries, resulting in an ambiance of iron hardness. On first sight, the visitor will find that this is no cordial, easygoing town, but it sure has character. Thriving in the Middle Ages, Gubbio at one time had a population of 50,000; the proud town fought often with neighbors, and once in a while rebelled against lords who tried to dominate it.

Many houses have a narrow secondary opening near the main entrance. It is known as the door of the dead, and is usually closed or even walled up. You are told it is opened only to allow the coffin of a deceased inhabitant to be carried out of the house. In olden times candles were lit outside those subsidiary doors on November 2, All Souls' Day, to help the souls in purgatory, who on that day were believed to be on leave, to find their former homes for a nostalgic visit.

Actually those small second entrances, their thresholds usually a few inches above the level of the street or sidewalk, may have been meant as a separate access to the upper floors while the street door was mainly for ground-floor shops and storerooms. A few old houses in Assisi, Spello, and Orvieto too have the narrow extra doors, but in Gubbio they are numerous.

Arriving from Perugia, the visitor passes modern housing

developments, garages, and service stations in the plain at the approaches to the hill, and enters the walled old town at the Piazza dei Quaranta Martiri (Square of the Forty Martyrs). The name is a tribute to forty hostages whom the retreating Nazis executed in June 1944 as a reprisal for the killing of a German officer and the wounding of one of their soldiers by local partisans.

The central Via della Repubblica and the other, narrower, lanes that link the five longitudinal and straight main streets are very steep. Souvenir shops next to the usual Umbrian ceramics stores display articles that I haven't seen in any other place in the region: small whips and tiny cudgels with a spiked metal ball on a chain (called morning stars in the Middle Ages when big versions were used as weapons). Is there a market for flagellation or sadism among the tourists coming to Gubbio?

I asked several people in Perugia and other parts of Umbria about those models of torture instruments. They all had the same ready explanation: The Gubbians (they didn't say *eugubini*), as everybody knows, "are all crazy." I had heard similar matter-of-fact remarks about the alleged weirdness of Gubbio natives before. It is a statistical fact—which may or may not be relevant in this connection—that Gubbio has one of the highest suicide rates in Italy. The town's relative isolation in a remote corner of Umbria and the dourness of the urban environment may be conducive to depression.

The dark medieval houses on the narrow streets and the implications of the many "doors of the dead" aren't exactly cheerful, it must be admitted, although they ooze plenty of atmosphere. From the upper end of the severe Via della Repubblica a stairway leads up to a remarkable complex of public buildings from the Middle Ages that seem to glower on the town below.

The edifices and the square around which they stand rest on powerful, arched foundations; the sharply rising slope of Mt. Ingino with its evergreen trees and shrubs and a church near its top provides an impressive backdrop. Every December the town illuminates the outline of a pine, several hundred feet tall, with colored electric bulbs on the flank of its mountain—the world's biggest Christmas tree, Gubbio claims.

The rectangular Piazza della Signoria, supported by four giant arches, is open at its northwestern side, offering from its parapet the panorama of the roofscape and church steeples below, the suburbs deeper down, the vast plain with its gardens and fields, and a string of green hills on the horizon.

On the north side of the square is the Palazzo dei Consoli (Palace of the Consuls), named after local magistrates who bore that title. The crenellated Gothic structure with a tower was erected in 1332–46 by Matteo di Giovanello of Gubbio whose surname was Gattapone; the elaborate portal is the work of Angelo da Orvieto, a contemporary of Gattapone. One of the busiest and most resourceful architects of the thirteenth century, Gattapone did much work also for Cardinal Albornoz, including the fortress of Spoleto (p. 101), his largest project.

The Palace of the Consuls is today the seat of the Civic Collections (Museo e Pinacoteca Comunale). The visitor climbs a high outer stairway and enters an enormous hall that takes up almost the entire lower floor of the building. It is large enough to have held the entire popular assembly when Gubbio was an independent state before the Duke of nearby Urbino, other overlords, and eventually the pope controlled the town.

Now the hall contains Roman antiquities and medieval sculptures. A few steps, left, lead to the much smaller gallery room of the Eugubine or Iguvine Tablets. They are one of the most important historical treasures in the region, an invaluable document for understanding the language, institutions, and religion of the ancient Umbrians.

The seven bronze sheets, some with greenish oxidation spots, are displayed in modern wooden frames so that they can be turned around. They are of unequal size—four large and three smaller ones, about the formats of a regular newspaper and of a tabloid. The larger tablets are inscribed with Etruscan and Latin letters on either side; the Etruscan lines are read right to left, the Latin ones left to right. The texts are all in the Umbrian language, which is related to, but not identical to, archaic Latin. Scholars theorize that the tablets are copies of fourth-century-B.C. texts made between the third and the first centuries B.C. when the Umbrians, writing in their own idiom, shifted from the Etruscan to the Latin alphabet.

The tablets were discovered near the ruins of the Roman Theater of Gubbio (p. 169) in 1444. The bronze slabs were originally nine, but two were sent to Venice for interpretation and never came back; they seem to have vanished. The town of Gubbio bought the remaining seven tablets in 1456 from the finder, a certain Paolo di Gregorio, in exchange for pasturage rights.

Paleographists completely deciphered and translated the Umbrian texts in the nineteenth century. They are essentially rules concerning the rituals to be observed in sacrificing animals—which liturgical objects are to be used and which divinities to be venerated. Jupiter and Mars but also other gods are named, and the wording of some prayers is prescribed. The religious practices had apparently been codified at a time when Gubbio was an

Umbrian city-state, influenced by Etruscan civilization, and through it acquainted with Greek mythology.

A steep staircase, its first flight open to the huge lower hall, mounts to the picture gallery; it's like climbing the many steps to a fourth-floor apartment. Several of the paintings shown are by unidentified minor masters of the Umbrian School, many of them transferred from churches in the town and district. Step onto the airy outer loggia with its marvelous panorama, the Roman ruins in the foreground.

The Palace of the Consuls faces the Palazzo Pretorio (Palace of the Magistracy) across the square, also designed by Gattapone. It is now Gubbio's Town Hall. A neoclassical, lengthy building on the northeast side of the piazza, the Palazzo Ranghiasci-Brancaleoni, is from the nineteenth century, a dignified addition to one of the great urban settings in Italy.

Farther up, on the highest spot of the steep town, is the cathedral; the fourteenth-century edifice was built so close to the slope of Mt. Ingino that the walls of the apse are in part embedded in the ground. The interior is adorned with pictures by local painters, mostly from the sixteenth century.

Opposite the cathedral is the Ducal Palace (Palazzo Ducale), a Renaissance building erected in 1476 for the brilliant Federico da Montefeltro of Urbino. The Montefeltro dukes were also lords of Gubbio between 1384 and 1631, and the local residence that Federico built for himself was a replica, on a smaller scale, of the splendid Montefeltro castle in Urbino. It has a colonnaded court-yard like the Urbino palace, which had been started under Duke Federico thirty years earlier.

In his Gubbio mansion Federico, the quintessential Renaissance man, wanted also a copy of his Urbino *studiólo*. This small study of a learned, book-loving ruler (who was also a commander of mercenary troops) with its delicately inlaid paneling of more than a dozen different kinds of wood and with its trompe-l'oeil effects is today still a major attraction of the Urbino palace. Instead, the Gubbio *studiólo* was dismantled long ago to decorate an aristocratic villa near Rome, and was eventually acquired by the Metropolitan Museum in New York. After thorough restoration, the *studiólo* of Gubbio has been on display in the New York institution since 1996.

In the upper part of Gubbio the small, early fifteenth-century Church of Santa Maria Nuova too rates a visit because of the well-preserved Madonna del Belvedere, the masterpiece of Ottaviano Nelli of Gubbio (1403). The harmonious composition shows the Virgin Mary, enthroned with the Infant Jesus, two saints, angels, and two kneeling members of the Pinoli family of Gubbio, who commissioned the work. The vivid colors and the sweet expressions of the Madonna and the music-playing angels make the picture an outstanding achievement of the Umbrian School.

Nelli frescoed also other churches in his native town besides working in Foligno, Umbértide, and Urbino. Frescoes by him or a disciple were discovered in 1942 in the apse of the Church of San Francesco in the low part of Gubbio, off the Square of the Forty Martyrs. The paintings include a Coronation of Mary and a History of the Virgin cycle.

The austere, dark-brown Franciscan church, with a hexagonal bell tower, was built at the end of the fourteenth century on the spot where St. Francis was said to have found a refuge after having broken with his father. According to tradition, three brothers of the influential Spadalonga family of Gubbio took the homeless young man in, and he would stay in the town for some time before establishing his first community in the Portiuncula near Assisi.

⌣ᐧ Saint and Wolf ᐧ⌣

St. Francis returned to Gubbio and preached in the town around 1220. The legend of his encounter with the Wolf of Gubbio is one of the most famous incidents of Umbrian lore: It seems that the town was then being terrorized by a huge, man-eating wolf. During one of St. Francis's outdoor sermons the scary animal, seeing a crowd of people, ran toward the saint with its jaws wide open. St. Francis made the sign of the cross, exclaiming: "Come hither, Brother Wolf; I command thee in the name of Christ to harm neither me nor anybody else!" (*Fioretti*, XXI).

The animal obeyed, and St. Francis sternly addressed it: "Thou art worthy of being hanged like a robber or murderer," but promised that if the wolf made peace with Gubbio "neither man nor dog shall pursue thee anymore." The wolf put its paw into the saint's hand in sign of a pledge, and from that day on lived for two years in the town, would go from house to house to ask for food from the people, and no dog barked after it. There was general mourning after the converted wolf died of old age. The small eighteenth-century Church of San Francesco della Pace (St. Francis of Peace) in the upper northeastern part of the town is said to mark the spot where the wolf that had made its peace with the town used to retire for the night after its daily rounds. A stone displayed in the church is supposed to have served as a pulpit for St. Francis during his open-air sermons.

Some 300 yards west of the lower Church of St. Francis are the ruins of a large Roman theater from the era of Emperor Augustus.

It could hold 16,000 spectators, its size proving the prominence that ancient Iguvium must have enjoyed. Now, classical drama is performed in the theater every summer.

The most exciting time in Gubbio's year, however, comes earlier, on May 15 and 16. This is the feast of St. Ubaldus, the heavenly patron of the town; it is boisterously celebrated every year, attracting crowds from all over Umbria as well as many other Italians and foreign tourists. Yet it isn't artificial or revival folklore but stirs genuine passions in the local people, as does the Palio race in Siena.

St. Ubaldus was Ubaldo Baldassini (1090–1160), the town's bishop for thirty-one years. More than that, he was also a civic leader and something of a military counselor. In 1154 his tactical advice saved Gubbio from an attack by a coalition of pro-papal (Guelph) neighboring cities including Perugia, Spoleto, and Città di Castello. The beloved and shrewd bishop told the commanders of the town's forces to move stealthily across the mountains north of Gubbio and outflank the besiegers. When the enemy troops learned of approaching columns they believed that a strong allied force was coming to the succor of Gubbio, and precipitously withdrew. The defenders pursued them, inflicting heavy losses. The jubilant people of Gubbio were convinced the victory was a miracle performed by their spiritual guide.

In 1155 the aged bishop went to the nearby Castle of Gualdo Tadino to plead with Emperor Frederick I Barbarossa to renounce the heavy tribute that he had imposed on Gubbio, and to spare the town. Ubaldo may have been advantaged by the circumstance, noted by his biographers, that his own ancestors were Germans who had come to Umbria with imperial troops. At any rate, Barbarossa relented and reconfirmed imperial privileges that

Gubbio had been granted earlier. Bishop Ubaldo died on May 16, 1160, and was canonized by Pope Celestine III in 1192.

The grateful Gubbians built a basilica as a burial place for St. Ubaldus at 2,600 feet altitude on the slope of Mt. Ingino two years after his canonization. The church was enlarged in later centuries. Curiously, a town in the French Alsace, Thann, also possesses a relic of the saint, which is supposed to have been smuggled out of Gubbio after his death by his German servant. Ubaldo is Theobald in German and Thibaut in French; the Alsatian church sharing the saint with the basilica on Mt. Ingino is known as St. Theobald's.

What's more, St. Ubaldus is entitled to reverence all over the world, at least by boxers. The Vatican has proclaimed him their patron saint because in his sermons he had exhorted the men in his flock to use their fists instead of their swords if during an argument they felt they had to fight. On the seventh centenary of the saint's death in 1960 Gubbio inaugurated a cableway from the upper part of the town to the Basilica of St. Ubaldus above it.

◡ Candle Race ∾

The festivities marking the anniversary of St. Ubaldus's death every year culminate in the so-called Race of the Candles (Corsa dei Ceri), an event that must have contributed to the Gubbians' reputation for being cracked. The "candles" are three contraptions of dark wood, twenty to twenty-three feet tall, consisting of two octagonal prisms each, crowned with wax figures of three saints. The sculptures represent St. Ubaldus as protector of the guild of stonemasons and bricklayers (a posthumous function much older than his heavenly protectorship of boxers); St. George as protector of merchants; and St. Anthony the Abbot as protector of the peasantry. During the year the three "candles" are kept in the Basilica of St. Ubaldus on Mt. Ingino from which they are taken into the town on the first Sunday in May.

In the morning of May 15 the town is awakened by drummers. The attendants of each of the three "candles," known as *ceraioli* (candlemen) gather around their sword-carrying commanders. The men wear colorful costumes—white trousers, a red sash, and gaudy shirts and caps that are yellow for the followers of St. Ubaldus, blue for those of St. George, and black for St. Anthony the Abbot. They have a ceremonial luncheon in the presence of the town authorities, and afterward the "candles" are raised into vertical position from the platforms on which they have been resting.

Bawdy shouts from the crowd always accompany this phallic episode. A jug filled with water is emptied at the bases of the "candles," and then thrown into the air; it breaks, and hundreds of people scramble to conquer one of the sherds. Figure out the symbolism. Then the wooden columns are paraded around the upper town and blessed by a prelate.

Toward evening the "candles" are again raised and taken into the Piazza della Signoria, which by then is filled with people. From the balcony of the Town Hall the mayor signals the start of the race. The athletic young men who have been training for the competition carry the swaying wooden columns at breakneck speed to the basilica high up on the slope. They run past the north side of the cathedral, and up the winding road to the top, climbing 900 feet, over one and a half miles, in about a quarter of an hour, a race requiring stout hearts and uncommon stamina. The "candles" remain in the mountain sanctuary for the next twelve months, whereas the wax figures topping them are carried back to town in a torch parade.

It seems that the memory of St. Ubaldus was honored with the race of the "candles" already a few years after his death, even before Rome proclaimed his sanctity. The event may have roots in much older pagan cults, possibly derived from prehistoric fertility rites. There is always a great deal of pushing and shoving during the St. Ubaldus celebrations; it's not gentle Umbria that the visitor experiences on that occasion. There is less horseplay and the mood is more relaxed on the two Sundays after May 15 when much smaller "candles" are carried in races by, respectively, teenagers and young boys.

The last Sunday in May is devoted in Gubbio to a crossbow-shooting contest. The target is put up against the facade of the Town Hall; the archers wear medieval costumes. Entrants from other towns, especially from an old rival, Sansepolcro in Tuscany, usually take part in the event, which is much more touristy than is the main Race of the Candles. All year round tiny crossbows can be bought at Gubbio's souvenir shops, where they are displayed side by side with those ominous models of whips and flails.

The Via Eugubina (National Route No. 298) proceeds from Gubbio's northwestern side through a narrow ravine to the Scheggia Pass (1,923 feet above sea level) and joins the Via Flaminia (National Route No. 3). An ancient Roman road station where horses were changed existed near the present village of Scheggia; in the Middle Ages pilgrims on their way to or from Rome found a hospice on the spot. From the Scheggia Pass it is thirty-six miles to Urbino and forty-six miles to the Adriatic Sea near Fano.

The rail stop closest to Gubbio is twelve miles distant, near

Fossato di Vico on the Rome-Ancona line; the station is officially called Fossato di Vico-Gubbio. Public buses run between Gubbio and the station. Fossato di Vico is a medieval village of 2,000 inhabitants, half of it in the plain, the other half on a hillside.

Five miles south of rural Fossato di Vico is Gualdo Tadino, a center of the ceramics industry on a slope above a fertile valley. An International Ceramics Exhibition is held in the town of 14,000 population every August and September; throughout the year an antiques market takes place on the second Sunday of each month. Gualdo Tadino was hard hit by the 1997–98 earth tremors.

The upper part of the town is close to a medieval fortress known as Rocca Flea (from the name of a little stream nearby). With its grim walls and keep it looks sinister enough to lend credit to the story that in the Renaissance the stronghold was the lair of robber barons who made a living by assailing travelers on the highway below; at one time its criminal occupants also counterfeited money.

In the plain, five miles from Gualdo Tadino, the Ostrogothic King Totila was defeated by the Byzantine eunuch Narses in A.D. 552. It was one of the decisive battles of the early Middle Ages. Totila with his Germanic forces had reconquered most of earlier Gothic possessions in Italy; subdued Sicily, Sardinia, and Corsica; captured and plundered Rome; and razed the walls of Spoleto, Perugia, and other Umbrian cities. Narses, the general of the Eastern Roman Emperor Justinian with his army, including Huns and Germanic allies, met the tens of thousands of Gothic warriors at a spot then known as Taginae or Tadinae. Totila's Ostrogoths were overwhelmed by the Byzantine archers and cavalry, and he himself was mortally wounded. The losers "transported their dying monarch seven miles beyond the scene of his disgrace," Gibbon writes, "and his last moments were not embittered by the presence of the enemy." The battle of Taginae virtually spelled the end of the Gothic kingdom in Italy. Totila's successor, Teja, and the remainder of the Gothic army would again be beaten by Narses in a battle below Mt. Vesuvius in 555, and the surviving Goths would be absorbed by the local population.

⌣ *Montefalco Vistas* ∿

A parapet on a salient outside one of the medieval town gates of entrancing Montefalco is the place to enjoy the panorama of a generous segment of the region: The broad, bountiful valleys of the Clitunno (Clitumnus) and Topino rivers, which converge near Foligno, are 750 feet below; the hill towns of Trevi and Spello greet like neighbors from across the street; Assisi and Perugia loom afar; on the slopes in the foreground are cypresses, rows of olive trees, and the vast vineyards where—only here—the renowned, strong Sagrantino wine is grown.

The vantage point with the celebrated sights has for centuries been known as the Balcony of Umbria (Ringhiera Umbra). The narrow street descending to it, from the main square of the little town of 5,500 people, is marked Via Ringhiera Umbra, and to Italians who know the town at all the sobriquet Balcony of Umbria springs to mind automatically the way "Eternal City" seems inevitable whenever the name Rome is pronounced.

On my latest trip to Montefalco, with friends, we didn't walk down at once to the "balcony"; we first paid a prolonged visit to San Francesco, the former Franciscan church higher up on the Via Ringhiera Umbra. It has long been a museum and is a major reason why anyone who wants to get the feel of Umbria must come to this town for at least half a day, possibly much longer. The deconsecrated Church of St. Francis, with famous frescoes by Benozzo Gozzoli and Perugino, has recently been expanded with a modern wing; there are now second-floor showrooms, a library, a new access to the crypt, and an elevator.

The choir of the old church with the Benozzo cycle is the museum's showpiece. The Florentine Benozzo di Lese (1420–97) became generally known by his nickname Gozzoli ("goiters" or "belly") only after his death. In Montefalco he signed himself "Benotii de Florentia" (Latin for Benozzo from Florence). He had worked as an assistant to Fra Angelico in Orvieto (p. 16) and Rome before; at the age of thirty he left the painting Dominican friar and came to Montefalco to work on his own. The Franciscans commissioned him to depict the history of their order's founder. The main apse of the Church of San Francesco, entirely frescoed by Benozzo in 1552, shows the saint in heavenly glory with medallions of his first thirteen disciples.

A dozen pictures represent episodes of the life and legends of St. Francis as told by the *Fioretti:* his birth, his gift of his cloak to a poor man, his sermon to the birds, his stigmata, his death, and others. One scene shows St. Francis blessing Montefalco. There are also portraits of popes, church fathers, cardinals, Dante, Petrarch, and Giotto. By Benozzo, furthermore, are the murals of the evangelists and various saints in a side chapel.

In a niche left of the church entrance are an Annunciation and a Nativity by Perugino (1515). The former church also contains several paintings by Francesco Melanzio (circa 1460–circa 1526), a native of Montefalco who rarely left the town. He had the opportunity to watch Benozzo Gozzoli and Perugino at work there, learning a lot from them.

The mayor of Montefalco, Luigi Gambacurta, is credited with saving the frecoes from major quake damage. After the first jolt in September 1997 the mayor, who teaches Italian literature at the local high school, inspected the museum, and found a small crack in the vault above the Benozzo works. He quickly called on local carpenters to erect scaffolding to protect the walls of the old church. The buttresses were hardly in place when a strong aftershock occurred, which caused much damage in Assisi and elsewhere; the Montefalco frescoes, however, were spared.

The works of art on display in showrooms in the sturdy modern annex of the former church suffered no harm during the emergency. They include more paintings by Melanzio that had been transferred to the museum from other churches in the town and in its surroundings.

Today acknowledged as a valid artist of the Umbrian School, the Montefalco painter must have thought of himself as essentially an artisan; he painted church banners and votive tablets for convents, religious confraternities, and private clients in his workshop between major commissions like decorating San Francesco's.

The restructured crypt of the former church contains ancient Roman and medieval sculptures and artifacts found at Montefalco and in its surroundings. The hill was demonstrably inhabited already by the old Umbrians, and was a Roman town, but hardly anything of its early history is known. It emerged in the Middle Ages as Curcurione (probably derived from some Roman name), a frontier fortress of the Lombard duchy of Spoleto.

The name Montefalco (Falcon Mountain), according to tradition, refers to a trained hunting falcon that Emperor Frederick I Barbarossa presented to local lords as a farewell gift after a sojourn in 1165. To this day the town's official coat of arms shows a black falcon on six stylized hills. Barbarossa's grandson, Emperor Frederick II, also visited Montefalco (1240); the imperial eagle and the Swabian cross, both in stone, crown the Gate of Frederick II across town from the Balcony of Umbria.

Today most visitors reach Montefalco in a fifteen-minute drive from Foligno, first across a level stretch of open land and then up a steep road with several bends between vineyards, entering the town through the Gate of St. Augustine. With its battlemented tower and high stone wall it is a dour, even menacing, entrance-way. Unfriendly people better keep out, it seems to warn. The gate opens to a rising, rather narrow, main street, officially called Corso G. Mameli, after Goffredo Mameli, the nineteenth-century Genoese patriot and poet who wrote the words of Italy's present national anthem. To local people the corso is simply "lo stradone" (the big street). Left and right, close to the town gate, are medieval palazzi with bare stones and brickwork sticking out and a few ancient Roman urns incorporated in the walls.

During our most recent visit we found several main-street shops offering Sagrantino (also spelled Sacrantino) wine, and lacework such as was once made by the local womenfolk, and now is machine-made. Oldsters were sitting and chatting or reading newspapers in no fewer than three barbershops on the stradone—obviously the tranquil town's social centers for men who want to get out of the house in the morning.

On the left side of the Corso G. Mameli, a few steps from the gate, is the 800-year-old Church of St. Augustine; the stark Gothic edifice harbors many faded frescoes from the fourteenth to the sixteenth centuries. Two glass-enclosed reliquaries located on either side of the nave will satisfy morbid tastes. In one, to the right, the draped skeletons of the Blessed Illuminata and the Blessed Chiarella, gilt crowns on their skulls, lie side by side. They both were Augustinian nuns, unrelated but close friends, who died in the early fourteenth century. Another glass chest on the left side contains the bones, clearly visible, of a Spanish pilgrim who is said to have been found dead in the church one morning centuries ago; he reportedly had been praying all night.

Past a couple of stately old palaces and narrow side lanes spanned by little arches the stradone leads up to the nearly circular main square, Piazza del Comune. Most conspicuous on it is the frescoed and porticoed Town Hall, which goes back to the thirteenth century but, owing to later changes and additions, looks much younger. The top of its tower commands an even vaster panorama than does the Balcony of Umbria outside the walls. A massive building opposite the Town Hall is the place where distinguished guests once would be put up; among them was the warrior Pope Julius II (1443–1513). A steep street between that palazzo and an arcaded house with a wine shop descends to the church-museum of San Francesco and the "balcony."

Half a dozen other churches in the little town would deserve to be visited too, as I found on earlier occasions, but several frescoes that had adorned them had meanwhile been transferred to the museum. We decided we had viewed enough art on a long morning, and adjourned to the restaurant of a simple hotel on the main street; unsurprisingly it is called Ringhiera Umbra.

When we ordered the pasta course of the day and the chicken, I teasingly asked the laconic woman manager what red wine she could recommend. She looked at me as if I were an alien from outer space, and said, "Sagrantino, of course." I had received the same answer in Norcia (p. 116). Drunk near the spot where it is grown, Sagrantino tastes superb. So good, indeed, that at a near-by wine shop I bought a bottle to take home. The owner advised: "When you open this bottle, wait for twenty minutes before drinking. Sagrantino needs time to breathe." Then I got a little lecture on Montefalco's own and exclusive vintage.

The vines that yield Sagrantino aren't very productive, it seems, requiring plenty of fertilizer and labor. Local vintners say their plants love their hills' calcareous soil, and if they thrive, which they do on the Montefalco hills in summer with plenty of sunshine, look majestic. Majestic? I wondered. "Yes, *maestoso*." The dark-red grapes, which have tough skins, are left to dry for forty days after harvesting before being pressed, to produce a "rather alcoholic, *generoso*, beverage."

If you haven't sampled too much of the *generoso* wine, you should drive from Montefalco another five miles northward to an even smaller hill town, Bevagna. It has a beautiful little piazza with two 800-year-old Romanesque churches, and an illustrious history, evidenced by the remains of a Roman theater and other ruins as well as by the antiquities in its small museum. Its Church of San Francesco, off the square, treasures a stone on which St. Francis is said to have rested his feet when he preached to the birds in a rural hollow somewhere near the town.

Giotto and Benozzo Gozzoli, among other artists, have pictured the legendary event, as told in the *Fioretti* (XVI): St. Francis is walking with some of his friars between Bevagna and the riverside village of Cannara when they notice a multitude of birds on the trees a little off the road. The saint steps into a field and starts preaching to the birds on the ground; those in the trees at once join them, and all listen attentively. "My little sisters, the birds!" St. Francis addresses them, evidently assuming they are all females (although the Italian word for bird, *uccèllo,* has the male gender).

"You owe much to God, your creator, and you ought to sing His praise," St. Francis tells his feathered congregation. "He has given you freedom to fly about, and though you neither spin nor sew He has given you twofold and threefold clothing. . . . He feeds you although you neither sow nor reap." The birds, according to the naïve story, open their beaks, stretch their necks, spread their wings, and bow their heads; they fly away only after the saint has dismissed them. In the air the flock forms into the shape of a cross, and the birds disappear in the directions of the four cardinal points.

People in various places around Bevagna insist that St. Francis preached to the birds in their own, specific neighborhood; a modern little sanctuary in a low-lying meadow near Cannara, known as Pian d'Arca, stakes a claim for that precious spot.

↔ Todi's Expatriates ↔

In the 1980s *Newsweek* magazine proclaimed Todi the most livable town in the world. "That article did us more harm than good," commented a native of the panoramic hill town who for the last twenty years has been working for the municipality. "Lots of Americans with lots of money invaded us," she explained. "They bought up apartments and houses in town, and old farmhouses in the countryside all around. Real estate prices went up steeply. Now you cannot find almost any *casolare* near Todi, and if you do the price is prohibitive, and you will have to spend three times as much to fix it up." A *casolare* is a rural building that has long been abandoned by its former inhabitants and often is dilapidated.

Americans who bought themselves a place in or near Todi in the 1970s got a bargain, and they aren't too happy either about the more recent rush of expatriates. If you sit at a café table in the main piazza today you invariably overhear English spoken all around. The business sign of a real estate agency, also in that square, reads MY HOUSE (although it's by no means easy now to find a house of your own in or near Todi). To facilitate communication between the natives and the newcomers, a local language school offers "full-immersion" English classes. American English is the lingua franca here; the British have for generations bought into Tuscany, so much so that the wine-growing Siena district is nicknamed "Chiantishire." While there is a scattering of British settlers around Todi too, the Americans are present in force, and coteries of Californians, New Yorkers, and Washingtonians have sprung up.

⌇ *Farmhouse-cum-Arsenal* ⌇

A new part-time resident who doesn't mingle much with Todi's expatriate crowd, Karen, is a close friend of mine; she bought a *casolare* a few miles south of the town in the early 1990s. The young Californian had been living in Rome as a journalist for years during the 1980s. She mentioned several times to me she was toying with the idea of acquiring some property in the Italian countryside, maybe a secluded ruin that she could transform into a retreat for herself and possibly for a future family (she was still single).

By then wealthy Americans, agents, successful artists, and millionaires from Milan were already swarming all over the hills around Todi, looking for decrepit farmhouses and castles, and prices had begun their meteoric rise. Karen joined the real estate search rather late, at the end of the 1980s, but had the advantages of fluency in Italian, of experience in Italian ways, and of being assisted by a knowledgeable Italian friend, a Roman architect who was doing work on some restoration projects in the area, including one for himself.

During the following two years the pair combed the surroundings of Todi and saw various properties. Karen, who had some money, eventually settled on one they had visited in their first reconnaissance trip. It was in a small cluster of stone farmhouses perched on a knoll in one of the valleys fanning out from Todi. Most of the *casolari* there were built with stones left in heaps when a twelfth-century village went up in flames, maybe in the course of some raid or military action. A few vestiges of the medieval settlement have survived. One is a handsome tower with a buttressed foundation and a steep stairway framed by flowerpots that the current owner, a retired Englishwoman, tends; before Karen came she was the only foreigner in the hamlet. There are also odd segments of the walls that once girded the village, and the slender campanile of its church, propped up by massive iron and wooden beams.

Karen and her architect friend inspected a house that had been deserted for years. Its tumble-down facade was graced by a portico and a tangle of grape vines; inside there was even running water and some electric wiring, proof that the *casolare* had been inhabited until not too long ago. Right away the architect warned Karen that the plumbing and everything else would have to be ripped out and the roof replaced because in a restoration the entire structure was to be gutted like a fish readied for the grill. The smell on the ground floor was overpowering—the farm animals had been kept in it, as was typical for such rural dwellings in old times.

What impressed Karen most on her first visit was a discovery she and her friend made when they clambered through a thicket of brambles and jumped over piles of stones in the back of the house. They found the remains of medieval walls crisscrossing the land that went with the property, and a tiny tower overgrown with ivy. Peering through the branches of trees bordering the house they could see Todi and its Renaissance jewel, the domed Church of Santa Maria della Consolazione (p. 193). What a perfect site for a romantic garden! That vista eventually was the clincher.

Only seven years later when Karen was married with two small children and living in London, that garden was at last taking shape. The intervening years had been taken up by arduous efforts, first to buy the property from two feuding (but related) families and then to see its rehabilitation through bureaucratic tangles and the tribulations of building. Karen, who owns an apartment in Rome, came to Italy from time to time to keep her Umbrian project going. I didn't see much of her during those years, but between rare meetings she told me in vivid letters how things were proceeding.

The first challenge for Karen was to bring together two neighbors in the hamlet who were cousins but weren't on speaking terms; each of them owned a half of the property, which was divided by a three-foot-thick stone wall. That wall explained why the *casolare* hadn't been already snapped up by somebody else:

Nobody wanted to pay a small fortune for half a country home. Karen must have exercised remarkable diplomatic skill in several meetings with one or the other of the coowners in a nearby tavern. The woman cousin claimed that her portion of the property was worth much more than the half belonging to her aged male relative, which, of course, he hotly disputed.

At last a price and the proportion of how the money was to be split between the two were agreed upon. Karen persuaded the hostile cousins to sit down with her around a table in the office of a notary public in Todi, and a contract was drawn up and signed. Later Karen found that the female cousin and her husband had surreptitiously removed valuable terra-cotta roof tiles that at the time of the signing were still in place. Well, such things will happen, she thought.

Then Karen had to deal with the Superintendency of Fine Arts (*Belle Arti*) in Perugia, the regional capital, concerning two ivy-draped jagged walls, the remains of a tower. The *Belle Arti* office, acting in the way of a national landmarks commission, wanted to investigate those stony fragments. "There is no historical or aesthetic grounds for this interest," Karen wrote me. "Italy is chock-a-block full of much more imposing ruins. What happened is that in registering the now unified property I had insisted that anything remotely resembling a ruin be included in the drawings I filed with the application. I wanted to make sure that if we (or our children with fresh funds) wanted to work on the tower or cottage the structures would be on record. Turns out the tower wasn't in the regional records dating back a century. The *Belle Arti* architects wanted to make sure Italy wasn't relinquishing one of its medieval treasures. This process took six months, much of them spent rescheduling missed appointments for on-site inspections." The

wait showed at least that Umbria's official conservationists were
taking their job seriously.

Construction start on the site was delayed also because the
contractor was busy with other projects in the area. Karen's first
baby was almost due when bulldozers and cranes with their crews
appeared on her Umbrian property to begin gutting the *casolare*
and tearing up the land. Digging inside the building had to be
done by hand, among other things to clear away the stones from
a collapsed oven in which bread once used to be baked.

Work was a year behind schedule and, Karen said, way over
budget when she, her husband, who is a television producer, with
their two-and-a-half-year-old son and a four-month-old baby girl
came to Italy from London to spend their first summer in their new
country home. "Actually we languished in Rome for several weeks
while workmen built the kitchen, painted the walls, installed the
toilets and tubs, and tiled the showers," Karen reported. "When
we finally moved in several windows were still missing."

"That first summer in the hamlet," she went on, "was more
memorable for its mishaps and the maelstrom of construction
than as the idyllic family home we had dreamed of. The house
was magnificent, all our friends who came told us. But it would
have looked even better without the never-ending parade of elec-
tricians, plumber,s and other brawny workmen who paid daily visits. And surely we would have enjoyed the stunning views of the
Umbrian countryside more with just the background hum of the
cicadas instead of the roar of the bulldozers and cement mixers
working on the pool for the next two months."

One morning the contractor, personally operating a bulldozer,
hit a cache of World War II explosives and nearly blew himself up

along with Karen and her family, then inside the half-finished house. It seems the Germans during their hasty retreat in Umbria in early July 1944 abandoned stockpiles of grenades and nitro-glycerin, and somebody—maybe sensing an opportunity for future black market deals—stored them in metal canisters, hiding them at the back of the empty *casolare*. The Carabinieri were alerted, and three officers came to the site, cordoned off the tower ruin with flimsy red-and-white plastic tape and announced they would summon explosives experts.

"Three weeks later," Karen wrote me, "when we had all but forgotten our arms cache, the bomb squad showed up while we were having breakfast with some house guests. I asked the officer who came to the door to kindly wait a moment since we thought it prudent to gather the four children we had between us and take a walk while his men disposed of the buried explosives. But by the time we got to the front door, they were already digging away. I had envisioned experts clad in special gear who would gingerly unearth the canisters, but there they were with pick and shovel." They removed the dangerous stuff all right, though.

By degrees the former *casolare* became a home. "There are the imcomparable sights of the Umbrian hills covered with golden fields of alfalfa hay," Karen wrote in one of her letters. "Sunflowers in full bloom, clumps of oaks and leafy vineyards bearing the first clusters of grapes just beyond the craters left by the bulldozers around the house. Not least there is a neighbor without whose help we would have been lost that first summer. A stout woman in her fifties, she cheerfully put up with all the chaos and helped us with housework and the children, and occasionally surprised us with homemade jam or tagliatelle."

Karen discovered that nearly all of her neighbors were related, ever bickering among themselves, but generally gracious to the American newcomers. A local farmer brought a crate piled with cucumbers and tomatoes from his kitchen garden, his way of saying welcome. His aunt lives next door to Karen's place, keeping six big dogs, more than a dozen chickens, and scores of pigeons. Whenever she doesn't disappear into the fields wielding a large stick to accompany her brood of chickens or collects firewood in the nearby thickets, she can be seen preparing endless pots of food, presumably mostly for her animals, or shelling peas on her doorsteps.

While Karen's next-door neighbor supplies her with fresh eggs from what must be some of Umbria's freest-range chickens, the barking dogs are a nuisance. The neighbor's son, a middle-aged civil servant, visits from time to time and takes out the pack for hunting wild boar, which still live near Todi together with foxes, rabbits, and quail.

In her latest letter Karen wrote: "We have almost grown used to the dogs' baying. It is mostly confined to meal times and when strangers come around. At least we don't have to worry about *ladri* [thieves], the bane of country-home owners owners in Umbria and Tuscany."

⌣ Triple-Wall Town ∾

Among the many charms of Todi proper are its lovely vistas due to the town's position on an isolated, steep ridge more than 700 feet above the valley of the Tiber. The river here turns to the southwest in a 90-degree bend, flows below Todi's northern flank, and a little downstream receives the water of the Naia. The location drew settlers to the ridge from prehistoric times. The hilltop town has been uninterruptedly inhabited for close to 3,000 years; today it numbers 17,000 residents, not counting the owners of vacation homes who come and go.

Todi is about halfway between Umbria's two main cities, twenty-five miles from Terni and twenty-eight miles from Perugia on Superhighway E-45, and to visit the town it's good to go by car. Todi can be reached from either city also by the Central Umbrian Railway (FCU, p. 65), but its diesel trains are slow and infrequent; sometimes buses substitute for them. From either one of Todi's two rail stations, Porta Rio or Porta Naia, the traveler still has to get to town over two miles of winding uphill highways; the public bus service isn't always reliable.

Arriving by car, the visitor will have to look for parking space outside the town walls—the outermost ones, that is. Ancient Todi is enclosed by three separate, concentric systems of fortifications, erected centuries apart as the town kept expanding. Walking to the center over sharply rising streets, one successively passes the gates of medieval, ancient Roman and Etruscan walls; it's like striding backward into early history.

The oldest surviving defenses went up in the fifth or fourth century B.C. when the hilltop settlement was inhabited by Umbrian farmers and artisans and an Etruscan aristocracy; it was then called Tuder or (on its coins) Tutere. The fact that the town struck its own coins attests to its early prominence. The main passage across the Etruscan walls is known as the Porta Marzia, or Mars Gate; the god of war seems to have had a conspicuous role in Todi's ancient cults. In 1835 a nearly life-size bronze statue of Mars from the fifth century B.C. was found in Todi. The Etruscan sculpture, which shows influences from contemporary Greek art, is now in the Vatican's Gregorian Museum of Pagan Antiquities. In 1996 a local civic group donated to the town a copy of that Mars statue, to be displayed in a long-planned Etruscan-Roman Museum of Todi.

Behind its three encircling walls, Todi occupies a triangle on the top of its hill. Narrow streets, stairways, and arched passages rise and descend on all sides. The stroller may suddenly see a tiny garden behind a dark brown ancient house, or from beneath a somber archway catch a glimpse of the arcadian countryside deep below and the green hills on the horizon. Water trickles from little medieval spouts or fountains in twisting lanes and dreamy squares. In winter it may be bitter cold on some days, and when it snows, which happens rarely, Todi looks like the illustration for a fairy tale.

Mounting from the medieval gate, the Porta Romana, in the southeastern corner of Todi, to the ancient Roman Gate of the Chains to the Etruscan Mars Gate a little behind it and farther up to the town core is a strenuous half-mile climb. At its end the visitor may feel short of breath but is rewarded by the sight of one of the most striking medieval squares in the entire country.

To the north is the quadrilateral Gothic facade of the nearly 900-year-old cathedral. Twenty-nine broad steps lead up to the three entrances under one big and two smaller rose windows. On the right side is a short, square bell tower. The inside of the large church, under the rafters of the wooden roof, looks bare. The inner side of the facade, opposite the main altar, is covered with a huge Last Judgment by Ferrau da Faenza (1562–1645) that is clearly inspired by Michelangelo's powerful fresco in the Vatican's Sistine Chapel. Flecks of badly damaged Trinity frescoes by Lo Spagna (1525) are visible in a side chapel.

The east side of the central square, Piazza del Popolo, is mostly taken up by two adjoining Gothic structures, both from the thirteenth century, the Palace of the Captain and the battlemented Palace of the People. An arched outdoor stairway, added later, links the two public buildings, which today serve jointly as the Town Hall. The Palace of the People houses a small picture gallery with a Coronation of the Virgin by Lo Spagna (1511); an adjacent collection, to be developed into a museum, contains prehistoric bronzes, Etruscan sculptures and coins, and other antiquities.

The south side of the Piazza del Popolo is occupied by the severe fourteenth-century Palace of the Priors with a crenellated flat roof, a square tower, and Renaissance windows. High up on the facade is a bronze eagle, the heraldic symbol of Todi. The small Piazza Garibaldi, opening from the main square between the Palace of the Priors and the Palace of the People, ends with a panoramic parapet at its east side. From it the cars and trucks on the superhighway and the other roads below look look like scurrying ants and the rare FCU train like a caterpillar. To the east are villages and hills.

On the west side of the piazza are a few stores and a café with many outdoor tables, often occupied by resident expatriates and tourists. A marble tablet on the eighteenth-century palace close to the cathedral records that the poet Paolo Rolli (1687–1763) lived in it. His claim to fame is that he was the first to translate Milton into Italian after having served as a preceptor of princes at the court of King George II of Britain. When his protectress, Queen Carolina, died in 1737, Rolli retired to Todi where he became a town character and an occasional butt of raillery because of his deviant way of life.

At the right side of the cathedral the Via del Duomo leads to the former, large seminary, built by Vignola (Iacopo Barozzi, p. 140). Today a restructured section of the complex is Todi's Palace of the Arts, a cultural and convention center. Every spring an Antiques Fair of regional importance is held here.

Walk south from the main square to the nearby Piazza della Repubblica, from which a broad, theatrical flight of stairs, interrupted by a patch of greenery, leads up between trees to the vast Church of San Fortunato near the highest point of the town. Various architects took turns in the construction of the edifice between 1292 and the second half of the fifteenth century, but the Gothic facade remained incomplete in its upper part. Two Romanesque stone lions, their muzzles smoothed by the innumerable hands that rubbed them through the centuries, in front of the finely sculptured central portal are remnants of an earlier medieval church. The paintings and frescoes inside the luminous building aren't outstanding. Generations of visitors covered the walls of one of the side chapels with graffiti.

The crypt, accessible by stairs from the nave, holds the tomb of Friar Jacopone da Todi, one of the first Italian poets who wrote in the vulgar, the people's language, instead of in Latin. The tombstone gives the year of his death as 1296, but according to scholars he actually died in 1306. Jacopo dei Benedetti, later known as Jacopone ("Big Jacob") was born into a wealthy family in Todi around 1236, studied law at Bologna University, and established himself as a lawyer in his native Todi. After the death of his wife, a countess, in the collapse of a ballroom ceiling in 1268, Jacopone entered the Franciscan Order as a friar. He took sides in the clerical disputes of the times, was excommunicated for heresy by Pope Boniface VIII in 1297, spent years as a prisoner in the basement of a monastery, and was absolved by Pope Benedict XI in 1301. He remained a devout friar to his death.

Jacopone wrote poetry also in Latin and is the presumed author of the hymn *Stabat Mater*, describing the sorrows of the Virgin Mary by the Cross. His canticles in the idiom of the common people, essentially in the Umbrian dialect, are known as the *Laudi* (praises). They are dramatic, with quick changes of mood, sometimes tender, sometimes rough; their subjects range from the Passion of Christ to warnings against corruption in the church. One poem extols St. Francis, the "Beloved of God." (St. Francis himself wrote at least one canticle in Italian, as mentioned on p. 151.) Soon Dante, Italy's greatest poet—who too left works in Latin—would make the vernacular of Florence, not Umbria's, into the national standard language.

The tomb of Jacopone, immured in a wall, has by no means the place of honor in the crypt of San Fortunato's. At the center of the underground chamber stands a huge marble sarcophagus containing the remains of St. Fortunatus, who was bishop of Todi under Ostrogoth domination in the sixth century, and of other sainted men and women.

The former Franciscan monastery adjacent to the Church of San Fortunato is now a high school. Nearby is a park amid the ruins of the ancient Roman fortress that sat on the summit of the Todi ridge. A little lower, on a platform beneath the park and the southwestern tip of the town, rises the honey-colored pilgrimage church of Santa Maria della Consolazione. It is a nobly proportioned Renaissance edifice with a dome that seems a scale model of the majestic cupola of St. Peter's in Rome, and three half domes. Bramante (whose real name was Donato d'Agnolo, circa 1444–1514), an architect in charge of the construction of St.

Peter's in Rome before Raphael and Michelangelo, is believed to have contributed designs for the Todi church, which was built between 1508 and 1607. To me, Santa Maria della Consolazione always appeared elegant but cool, out of character with the Gothic architecture and medieval mood of the town above it.

Motorists driving on the highway from Todi to Orvieto, twenty-four miles distant, pass the Church of Santa Maria della Consolazione. A few miles farther, National Route No. 448 picturesquely coasts the Tiber and the artificial lake the river forms before it turns again south in another right angle. The reservoir, called Lake of Corbara, was built in 1958, is more than four miles long, and feeds a large power plant from a dam in front of the medieval Castle of Corbara. The hamlet of the same name, surrounded by old oaks, is administratively an out-lying suburb of Orvieto.

A little downstream, on a hill high above the Tiber, is the picturesque village of Baschi, its sixteenth-century parish church with a high, square steeple jutting heavenward out of a conical cluster of gray houses. Seeing this heap of old stones and masonry, one would hardly guess the once-remarkable role of the place. In Roman times a sumptuous villa occupied the hill, as many archeological finds prove. In the Middle Ages the Counts of Baschi from their castle—of which little has survived—controlled Tiber navigation, dominated a sizable territory, and allied themselves at times with Todi, at other times with Orvieto in their rivalries and wars.

Today the archaic-looking village on its seemingly precarious perch right above the Motorway of the Sun, National Route A-1, is a welcome landmark for travelers coming from the north: When they glimpse it high above a support wall on the left side of the autostrada they know it will take only one more hour to arrive in Rome. To motorists driving northward from the Italian capital, the unmistakable sight of Baschi instead signals that they are in Umbria and that one of the region's jewels, Orvieto, is near.

Appendix

Umbria Directory

The following pages list the major cities and towns described in this book, furnishing practical information. The American abbreviation ZIP is used for what in Italian is CAP (*codice di avviamento postale*); the five-digit figure precedes the place name in Italian addresses. TAC stands for telephone area code (in Italian: *prefisso*). Calling from abroad, dial 39, the international country code for Italy before the zero of the area code.

The letter I in the following listings means tourist information office. If you want to write to one of the addresses supplied under I, preface it with *Azienda di Promozione Turistica*.

The indications on how to reach the various places by car

recommend the most convenient routes, which are not necessarily the shortest by mileage. Motorway A-1, known as Autostrada del Sole (Motorway of the Sun), is a toll road. When traveling to any destination in Umbria from Rome, motorists conveniently take A-1 (north) as far as the Orte or Chiusi-Terme di Chianciano exits; for traveling to Umbria from Florence, Motorway A-1 (south) as far as the Arezzo or Valdichiana exits offers the best connections.

National routes are indicated by their official numbers. The word *bis* (Latin for "twice") after a highway number marks an alternate route. Some of the national routes are divided superhighways; E-45 is a national route and superhighway that is part of the European long-distance road network.

The travel times given for railroad trips assume the briefest waiting periods for connecting trains and, where necessary, for additional bus rides according to the official schedules.

Since admission times and fees for museums and other sights vary frequently, it is recommended to check beforehand by phone where a number is supplied. The admission to churches is generally free, but many are closed between one and three or four P.M., some also for longer periods. Visitors should abstain from loud talk, laughter, or other behavior that might be interpreted as irreverent, especially during religious services.

The hotels and restaurants mentioned here are marked with a (T) for top-rated, (M) for medium-range, and (P) for plain; quality, decor, service, and prices were considered. The author has personally investigated most of the establishments named, while relying on the recommendations of trusted and knowledgeable friends with regard to a few others.

$\mathcal{A}$melia (p. 77).

Altitude 1,332 feet (406 meters). Population: 11,200. ZIP 05022.
TAC 0744. I: Via Orvieto 1, tel. 981-453, fax 981-566.

SIGHTS.

Cyclopean walls. Panorama.

TO REACH AMELIA.

By road from Rome, 58 miles (93 kilometers) by Motorway A-1
to Orte, Superhighway Route 204 to Narni Scalo, and Route
205; from Florence, 143 miles (228 kilometers) by Motorway A-
1 (south) to Orte, proceeding as above. By rail from Rome to
Narni-Amelia station, and public bus from Narni to Amelia (6.8
miles or 11 kilometers) in little more than an hour; from
Florence via Orte (change of trains required) and Narni-Amelia
in two hours and ten to forty minutes.

HOTEL.

Anita (M), Via Roma 31, tel. 982-146, fax 983-079.

RESTAURANTS.

Carleni (M), Via P. Carleni 21, tel. 983-925 (dinner only). Anita
(M), Via Roma 31, tel. 982-146.

$\mathcal{A}$ssisi (p. 139).

Altitude 1,322–1,657 feet (403–505 meters). Population: 24,000. ZIP
06081. TAC 075. I: Piazza del Comune 12, tel. 812-534, fax 813-727.

SIGHTS.

Basilica of St. Francis with Giotto frescoes. Church of St. Clare.
Cathedral. Basilica of Santa Maria degli Angeli with Portiuncula

Chapel, 3 miles (5 kilometers) southwest of the town center. Temple of Minerva. Civic Picture Gallery (Pinacoteca Comunale), Piazza del Comune 1, tel. 812-579. Archeological Museum and Roman Forum, Via Portica, tel. 813-053. Fortress (Rocca Maggiore), tel. 815-292. Excursion to Hermitage of the Prisons (Eremo delle Prigioni), 2.4 miles (3.8 kilometers) east of the town center.

TO REACH ASSISI.

By road from Rome, 111 miles (177 kilometers) by Motorway A-1, Superhighway Route 204 to Terni, Route 3 to Foligno, and Superhighway Route 75; from Florence, 113 miles (180 kilometers) by Motorway A-1 (south) to Valdichiana, Superhighway Route 75-bis to Perugia, and Superhighway Route 75; from Perugia, 16 miles (26 kilometers) by Superhighway Route 75 (east). By regional bus (SULGA Company) from Rome, Tiburtina Bus Terminal, in three hours; from Florence, Piazza Adua, three hours. By rail from Rome, two hours and ten minutes to two hours and thirty minutes via Foligno (change of trains required at most times; from Florence, two hours and fifty minutes via Terontola-Cortona (change of trains required at some times); from Perugia, twenty minutes.

HOTELS.

Subasio (T), Via Frate Elia 2, tel. 812-206, fax 816-691. Giotto (T) Via Fontebella 41, tel. 812-209, fax 816-479. Umbra (M), Vicolo degli Archi 6, tel. 812-240, fax 813-653. Cristallo (M), Via Los Angeles, Santa Maria degli Angeli, tel. 804-3094, fax 804-3538. Porta Nuova (M), Viale Paul Sabatier 21, tel. 812-405, fax 816-539. Pallotta (P), Via San Rufino 4, tel. 812-649. Del Viaggiatore (P), Via Sant'Antonio 14, tel. 816-297, fax 813-051.

RESTAURANTS.

San Francesco (M), Via San Francesco 52, tel. 813-302. Taverna dell'Arco-Da Bino (M), Via San Gregorio 8, tel. 812-383. I Portici (P), Via Portica 29, tel. 815-126.

$\mathscr{B}$*ettona* (p. 63).

Altitude 1,158 feet (353 meters). Population: 3,500. ZIP 06084. TAC 075. I: Piazza del Comune 12, 06081 Assisi, tel. (075) 812-450, fax (075) 813-727.

SIGHTS.

Town walls. Panorama.

TO REACH BETTONA.

By car from Rome, 101 miles (162 kilometers) by Motorway A-1 to Orte, Superhighway Route 204 and Superhighway Route E-45 to Assisi-Santa Maria degli Angeli, and provincial highway (south); from Florence, 116 miles (186 kilometers) by Motorway A-1 (south) to Valdichiana, Superhighway Route 75-bis to Perugia, Superhighway Route E-45 (south) to Sant'Andrea d'Agliano, and provincial highway (east) for 7 miles (11 kilometers). By rail from Rome, three hours to Perugia via Orte and Foligno (change of trains required at most times), proceeding for 12 miles (19 kilometers) by public bus; from Florence, two hours and fifty minutes to Perugia via Terontola-Cortona (change of trains required at some times), proceeding by public bus, as above.

HOTEL.

Cinque Cerri (P), Località Malandruga 87, tel. 986-9173.

RESTAURANT.

La Fattoria (M), Via D. Fattoria, tel. 986-9240.

$\mathcal{B}$*evagna* (p. 180).

Altitude 689 feet (210 meters). Population: 4,600. ZIP 06031. TAC 0742. I: Piazza Garibaldi 12, 06034 Foligno, tel. (0742) 350-493, fax (0742) 340-545.

SIGHTS.

Church of San Francesco. Roman Theater. Bevagna Museum (Museo di Bevagna), Corso G. Matteotti 70, tel. 360-031.

TO REACH BEVAGNA.

By road from Rome, 103 miles (165 kilometers) by Motorway A-1 to Orte, Superhighway Route 204 to Terni, Route 3 to Foligno, and provincial highway (southwest) for 5 miles (8 kilometers); from Florence, 123 miles (196 kilometers) by Motorway A-1 (south) to Valdichiana, Superhighway Route 75-bis to Perugia, Superhighway Route 75 to Foligno, and provincial highway (southwest), as above. By rail from Rome to Foligno in two hours; from Florence in three hours via Terontola-Cortona (change of trains required at some times), proceeding by public bus over 5 miles (8 kilometers).

RESTAURANT.

Da Nina (M), Piazza Garibaldi 6, tel. 360-161.

$\mathcal{C}$*ascia* (p. 117).

Altitude 2,146 feet (645 meters). Population: 3,200. ZIP 06043. TAC 0743. I: Piazza Garibaldi 1, tel. 71-147, fax 76-630.

SIGHTS.

Basilica and Convent of St. Rita.

TO REACH CASCIA.

By road from Rome, 110 miles (176 kilometers), by Motorway
A-1 to Orte, Superhighway Route 204 to Terni, Route 209 to
Triponzo, and Route 320; from Florence, 172 miles (275 kilo-
meters) by Motorway A-1 (south) to Valdichiana, Superhighway
Route 75-bis to Perugia, Superhighway Route 75 to Foligno,
Route 3 to Spoleto, Routes 395 and 209 to Tripenzo, and Route
320. By rail from Rome in an hour and forty minutes to Spoleto,
proceeding by public bus for 32 miles (51 kilometers); from
Florence in three to four hours to Spoleto, proceeding by bus, as
above.

HOTELS.

Monte Meraviglia (M), Via Roma 15 A, tel. 76-142, fax 71-127.
Il Quadrifoglio (M), Via Cavour 1 A, tel. 76-900.

RESTAURANTS.

Il Tartufo (M), Via Roma 15 A, tel. 76-142. La Tavernetta (M),
Via G. Palombi 1, tel. 71-387. La Brace (M), Via Roma 32, tel.
76-015.

Castiglione del Lago (p. 29).
Altitude 997 feet (304 meters). Population: 13,000. ZIP 06061.
TAC 075. I: Piazza Mazzini 10, tel. 965-2484, fax 965-2763.

SIGHTS.

Medieval castle. Ducal Palace. Lake panorama.

To Reach Castiglione del Lago.

By road from Rome, 114 miles (182 kilometers) by Motorway A-1 to Chiusi-Terme di Chianciano and Route 71; from Florence, 79 miles (126 kilometers) by Motorway A-1 (south) to Valdichiana, Superhighway Route 75-bis to Borghetto, and Route 71 (south). By rail from Rome, two hours and ten minutes; from Florence, one hour and forty minutes.

Hotels.

Duca della Corgna (M), Via Buozzi 143, tel. 953-238, fax 965-2446. Miralago (M), Piazza Mazzini 6, tel. 951-157, fax 951-924.

Restaurants.

Miralago (M), Piazza Mazzini, tel. 951-157. La Cantina (M), Via Vittorio Emanuele 86, tel. 965-2463.

Città della Pieve (p. 24).

Altitude 1,670 feet (509 meters). Population: 6,600. ZIP 06062. TAC 0578. I: Piazza Mazzini 10, 06061 Castiglione del Lago, tel. (075) 965-2484, fax (075) 965-2763.

Sights.

Perugino frescoes in Church of Santa Maria dei Bianchi and in the cathedral. Perugino's birthplace, Via Pietro Vannucci. Medieval fortifications and panorama.

To Reach Città della Pieve.

By road from Rome, 106 miles (170 kilometers) by Motorway A-1 to Chiusi-Chianciano Terme and Route 71 (south); from Florence, 84 miles (134 kilometers) by Motorway A-1 (south) to

Chiusi-Chianciano Terme, and Route 71 (south). By rail from Rome, in two hours and fifteen minutes to Chiusi-Chianciano Terme, proceeding by public bus over 5 miles (8 kilometers); from Florence, in two hours to Chiusi-Chianciano Terme, proceeding by bus, as above.

HOTEL.

Vannucci (M), Via Icilio Vanni 1, tel. and fax 298-063

RESTAURANT.

Vannucci (M), as above.

Città di Castello (p. 67).

Altitude 945 feet (288 meters). Population: 38,000. ZIP 06012. TAC 075. I: Piazza Fanti, tel. 855-4922, fax 855-2100.

SIGHTS.

Civic Picture Gallery (Pinacoteca Comunale), Palazzo Vitelli alla Cannoniera, Via della Cannoniera, tel. 855-4202. Cathedral Museum (Museo del Duomo), Piazza Gabriotti 3 A, tel. 855-4705. Alberto Burri Collection, Palazzo Albizzini and former Tobacco Factory, tel. 855-4649.

TO REACH CITTÀ DI CASTELLO.

By road from Rome, 161 miles (258 kilometers) by Motorway A-1 to Orte, Superhighways Route 204 and Route E-45; from Florence, 77 miles (123 kilometers) by Motorway A-1 (south) to Arezzo, Route 73 to Sansepolcro, and Superhighway Route E-45 (south). By rail from Rome, four hours to Terni, proceeding by Ferrovia Centrale Umbra (FCU) local train; from Florence, seventy minutes to Arezzo proceeding by public bus over 26 miles (42 kilometers).

HOTELS.

Tiferno (T), Piazza Raffaello Sanzio 13, tel. 855-0331, fax 852-1196. Le Mura (M), Via Borgo Farinario. tel. 852-1070, fax 852-1350.

RESTAURANTS.

Il Bersaglio (M), Via Orlando 14, tel. 855-5534. Lea (P), Via San Florido 38, tel. 852-1678.

$\mathcal{D}$eruta (p. 64).

Altitude 715 feet (217 meters). Population: 7,600. ZIP 06053. TAC 075. I: Via Mazzini 21, 06100 Perugia, tel. (075) 572-5341, fax (075) 573-6828.

SIGHTS.

Ceramics Museum and Civic Picture Gallery, Piazza dei Consoli 1, tel. 971-1000.

TO REACH DERUTA.

By road from Rome, 96 miles (153 kilometers) by Motorway A-1 to Orte, and Superhighways Route 204 and Route E-45; from Florence, 109 miles (174 kilometers) by Motorway A-1 (south) to Valdichiana, Superhighway 75-bis to Perugia, and Superhighway Route E-45 (south); from Perugia, 12.5 miles (20 kilometers) by Superhighway Route E-45 (south). By rail from Rome in two hours and thirty minutes to Perugia, proceeding by public bus over 12.5 miles (20 kilometers); from Florence, two hours and ten to forty minutes to Perugia, and public bus, as above.

HOTELS.

Melody (M), kilometer 55.800 on Superhighway Route E-45, tel. 971-1186, fax 971-1018. Asso di Coppe (P), kilometer 73.400, Superhighway Route E-45, tel. 971-0205, fax 972-025.

RESTAURANT.

Il Patio (P), Via Tiberina 188/190, tel. 971-1564.

Foligno (p. 127).

Altitude 768 feet (234 meters). Population: 53,000. ZIP 06034. TAC 0742. I: Porta Romana 126, tel. 350-493, fax 350-545.

SIGHTS.

Palazzo Trinci with Picture Gallery (Pinacoteca), Piazza della Repubblica, tel. 3301 (four digits). Cathedral. Church of Santa Maria Infraportas.

TO REACH FOLIGNO.

By road from Rome, 99 miles (158 kilometers) by Motorway A-1 to Orte, Superhighway Route 204 to Terni, and Route 3; from Florence, 118 miles (189 kilometers) by Motorway A-1 (south) to Valdichiana, Superhighway Route 75-bis to Perugia, and Superhighway Route 75 (east). By rail from Rome in an hour and forty minutes; from Florence in about three hours via Terontola-Cortona (change of trains required at most times).

HOTELS.

Poledrini (M), Viale Mezzetti 2, tel. 341-041, fax 341-042. Le Mura (M), Via Bolletta 27, tel. 357-344, fax 357-345.

RESTAURANTS.

Ponte dei Cesari (M), Viale Venti Settembre 39, tel. 350-608.
Villa Roncalli (M), Via Roma 25, on southern outskirts, tel. 391-091.

Gualdo Tadino (p. 174).

Altitude 1,758 feet (586 meters). Population: 14,000. ZIP 06023.
TAC 075. I: Piazza Oderisi 6, 06024 Gubbio, tel. (075) 922-0693,
fax (075) 927-3409.

SIGHT.

Rocca Flea fortress.

TO REACH GUALDO TADINO.

By road from Rome, 121 miles (193 kilometers) by Motorway A-1 to Orte, Superhighway Route 204 to Terni, and Route 3; from
Florence, 127 miles (204 kilometers) by Motorway A-1 (south)
to Valdichiana, Superhighway Route 75-bis to Perugia, and
Route 318. By rail from Rome in two hours and twenty minutes;
from Florence in about four hours via Terontola-Cortona
(change of trains required at most times) and Foligno (change of
trains required).

HOTEL.

Gigiotto (M), Via Morone 5, tel. and fax 912-283.

RESTAURANTS.

Anna (M), Località Boschetto 2, tel. 810-171. Gigiotto (M), Via
Morone 5, tel. 912-283.

$\mathcal{G}ubbio$ (p. 159).

Altitude 1,568–1,736 feet (478–529 meters). Population: 31,000. ZIP 06024. TAC 075. I: Piazza Oderisi 6, tel. 922-0693, fax 927-3409.

SIGHTS.

Civic Museum with Eugubine Tablets, Palazzo dei Consoli Ducal Palace, tel. 927-5872. Medieval Town. Church of Santa Maria Nuova with Madonna del Belvedere by Ottaviano Nelli. Church of St. Francis with Nelli frescoes. Roman Theater. National Archeological Museum, Via Buozzi, tel. 922-0992.

TO REACH GUBBIO.

By road from Rome, 136 miles (217 kilometers) by Motorway A-1 to Orte, Superhighway Route 204, Superhighway Route E-45 via Perugia to Bosco, and Route 298; from Florence, 121 miles (193 kilometers) by Motorway A-1 (south) to Valdichiana, Superhighway Route 75-bis to Perugia, Superhighway Route E-45 (north) to Bosco, and Route 298; from Perugia, 24 miles (39 kilometers by Superhighway Route E-45 (north) to Bosco, and Route 298. By rail from Rome in two hours and thirty to fifty minutes to Fossato di Vico-Gubbio, and public bus over 12 miles (19 kilometers); from Florence in about four hours via Orte (change of trains required) to Fossato di Vico-Gubbio and public bus, as above.

HOTELS.

Park Hotel ai Cappuccini (T), Via Tifernate, tel. 9234 (four digits), fax 922-0323. Bosone Palace (M), Via Venti Settembre 22, tel. 922-0698, fax 922-0552; Gattapone (P), Via Giovanni Ansidei 6, tel. 927-2489, fax 927-1269.

RESTAURANTS.

Taverna del Lupo (T), Via della Repubblica 47, tel. 927-4368.
Alla Balestra (M), Via della Repubblica 46, tel. 927-3810.
Amadeus (P), Via Savelli della Porta 5, tel. 927-4732.

Montefalco (p. 175).

Altitude 1,552 feet (473 meters). Population: 5,500. ZIP 06036.
TAC 0742. I: Piazza Garibaldi 12, 06034 Foligno, tel. (0742) 350-
493, fax (0742) 340-545.

SIGHTS.

Panorama from "Balcony of Umbria." Civic Museum of St.
Francis with frescoes by Benozzo Gozzoli and works by other
masters of the Umbrian School, Via Ringhiera Umbra 6, tel.
379-598. Church of St. Augustine.

TO REACH MONTEFALCO.

By road from Rome, 91 miles (145 kilometers) by Motorway A-
1 to Orte, Superhighway Route 204 to Terni, Route 3 to Foligno,
and Route 316; from Florence, 126 miles (202 kilometers) by
Motorway A-1 (south) to Valdichiana, Superhighway Route 75-
bis to Perugia, Superhighway Route 75 to Foligno, and Route
316. By rail from Rome in a little more than two hours to
Foligno, proceeding by public bus over 7.5 miles (12 kilometers); from Florence in three hours to Foligno via Terontola-
Cortona (change of trains required at most times), proceeding
by public bus, as above.

HOTELS.

Villa Pambuffetti (M), Via della Vittoria 20, on the outskirts, tel. 378-503, fax 379-245. Ringhiera Umbra (P), Via G. Mameli 20, tel. and fax 379-166.

RESTAURANTS.

Coccorone (M), Largo Tempestivi, tel. 379-535. Ringhiera Umbra (M), Via G. Mameli 20, tel. 379-166.

Narni (p. 81).

Altitude 787 feet (240 meters). Population: 20,100. ZIP 05035. TAC 0744. I: Viale C. Battisti 5, 05100 Terni, tel. (0744) 423-047, fax (0744) 427-259.

SIGHTS.

Panorama of the Nera and Tiber valleys. Cathedral. Picture Gallery in former Church of San Domenico. Fortress.

TO REACH NARNI.

By road from Rome, 56 miles (89 kilometers) by Motorway A-1 to Orte, and Superhighway Route 204; from Florence, 134 miles (215 kilometers) by Motorway A-1 (south) to Orte and Superhighway Route 204. By rail from Rome about one hour to Narni-Amelia and public bus over 2.5 miles (4 kilometers); from Florence, two hours and thirty minutes to Narni-Amelia via Orte (change of trains required), and public bus, as above.

HOTEL.

Dei Priori (M), Vicolo del Comune 4, tel. 726-843, fax 717-259.

RESTAURANTS.

Il Minareto (M), Via dei Cappuccini Nuovi 32, tel. 726-344. La Loggia (M), Vicolo del Comune 4, tel. 722-744.

Norcia (p. 107).

Altitude 1,982 feet (604 meters). Population: 4,700. ZIP 06046. TAC 0743. I: Via G. da Chiavano 2, 06043 Cascia, tel. (0743) 71-401, fax (0743) 76-630.

SIGHTS.

Basilica of St. Benedict. La Castellina with Civic Museum (when reopened). Tempietto.

TO REACH NORCIA.

By road from Rome, 98 miles (157 kilometers) by Motorway A-1 to Orte, Superhighway Route 204 to Terni, Route 209 to Triponzo, Route 320 to Serravalle, and Route 396; from Florence, 166 miles (266 kilometers) by Motorway A-1 (south) to Valdichiana, Superhighway Route 75-bis to Perugia, Superhighway Route 75 (east) to Foligno, Route 3 (south) to Spoleto, Routes 395 and 209 to Triponzo, Route 320 to Serravalle, and Route 396. By rail from Rome in about two hours to Spoleto, proceeding by public bus over 30 miles (48 kilometers); from Florence in three to four hours to Spoleto via Orte (change of trains required), proceeding by bus, as above.

HOTELS.

Posta (M), Via C. Battisti 12, tel. and fax 817-434. Grotta Azzurra (P), Via Alfieri 12, tel. and fax 816-513.

RESTAURANTS.

Taverna del Boscaiolo (M), Via Bandera 9, tel. 816-355. Dal
Francese (M), Via Riguardati, tel. 816-290.

Orvieto (p. 3).

Altitude 1,066 feet (325 meters). Population: 21,000. ZIP 05018.
TAC 0763. I: Piazza del Duomo 24, tel. 341-772, fax 344-433.

SIGHTS.

Cathedral. Papal Palace and Cathedral Museum. Etruscan tombs.
Civic Museum Claudio Faina, Piazza del Duomo. Emilio Greco
Museum, Piazza del Duomo, tel. 344-605. Well of St. Patrick,
Viale Sangallo, tel. 343-768. Former Church of San Domenico.

TO REACH ORVIETO.

By road from Rome, 76 miles (121 kilometers) by Motorway A-
1; from Florence, 119 miles (191 kilometers) by Motorway A-1
(south). By rail from Rome in one hour and twenty minutes;
from Florence in two hours and fifteen minutes.

HOTELS.

Maitani (T), Via Maitani 5, tel. and fax 342-011. Aquila Bianca
(M), Via Garibaldi 13, tel. 341-246, fax 342-273. La Badia (T),
at hamlet La Badia, nearly 4 miles (6 kilometers) distant from
Orvieto, tel. (0763) 90-359, fax (0763) 92-796.

RESTAURANTS.

Trattoria Etrusca (M), Via Maitani 10, tel. 344-016. La Pergola
(M), Via dei Magoni 9 B, tel. 343-065. Del Moro (P), Via San
Leonardo 7, tel. 342-763.

$\mathscr{P}$assignano sul $\mathscr{T}$rasimeno (p. 33).

Altitude 984 feet (289 meters). Population: 4,700. ZIP 06065. TAC
075. I: Piazza Mazzini 10, 06061 Castiglione del Lago, tel (075)
965-2484, fax (075) 965-2763.

SIGHTS.

Lake Panorama. Boat trip to Isola Maggiore. Fishery Museum at
San Feliciano, Via Lungolago Alicata 23, tel. (075) 849-716.

TO REACH PASSIGNANO SUL TRASIMENO.

By road from Rome, 132 miles (211 kilometers) by Motorway A-
1 to Chiusi-Chianciano Terme, Route 71 (north) to Borghetto,
and Superhighway Route 75-bis; from Florence, 84 miles (134
kilometers) by Motorway A-1 (south) to Valdichiana and
Superhighway Route 75-bis; from Perugia, 18 miles (28 kilometers) by Superhighway Route 75-bis. By rail from Rome, two
hours and thirty minutes via Terontola-Cortona (change of
trains required at most times); from Florence, about two hours
via Terontola-Cortona (change of trains required at some times);
from Perugia in twenty-five minutes.

HOTELS.

Trasimeno (M), Via Roma 16 A, tel. 829-355, fax 829-267. Sauro
(M), on Isola Maggiore, tel. 826-168, fax 825-130.

RESTAURANTS.

Il Fischio del Merlo (M), Via Gramsci 14, tel. 829-283. Sauro
(M) on Isola Maggiore, tel. 826-168.

$\mathscr{P}erugia$ (p. 37).

Altitude 1,617 feet (493 meters). Population: 144,000. ZIP 06100. TAC 075. I: Piazza Quattro Novembre 3, tel. 573-6458, fax 573-6828.

SIGHTS.

Etruscan Arch and Walls. Cathedral. National Gallery of Umbria and Palazzo dei Priori, Corso Vannucci, tel. 572-0316. Collegio del Cambio, Corso Vannucci. Etruscan Well, Piazza Piccinino 1, tel. 573-3669. Rocca Paolina (fortress, with access from Piazza Italia). Church of San Severo with Raphael fresco. Oratory of St. Bernardine. Museum of the Academy of Fine Arts, Piazza San Francesco 5, tel. 572-6562. National Archeological Museum, Piazza G. Bruno 10, tel. 572-141. Panorama from south side of Prefecture. Church of San Pietro. Excursion to Tomb of the Volumnii (Ipogeo).

TO REACH PERUGIA.

By road from Rome, 108 miles (173 kilometers) by Motorway A-1 to Orte, Superhighway Route 204 and Superhighway Route E-45; from Florence, 96 miles (154 kilometers) by Motorway A-1 (south) to Valdichiana and Superhighway Route 75-bis. By rail from Rome in two hours to two hours and thirty minutes via Foligno or Terontola-Cortona (change of trains required at either station at certain times); from Florence in two hours and ten to forty minutes via Terontola-Cortona (change of trains required at some times).

HOTELS.

Brufani (T), Piazza Italia 12, tel. 573-2541, fax 572-0210. La Rosetta (M), Piazza Italia 19, tel. and fax 572-0841. Grifone (M), Via Silvio Pellico 1, tel. 583-7616, fax 583-7619. Signa (P), Via del Grillo 9, tel. 572-4180.

RESTAURANTS.

Osteria del Bartolo (T), Via Bartolo 30, tel. 573-1561. Ubu Re (M), Via Baldeschi 17, tel. 573-5461. La Rosetta (M), Piazza Italia 19, tel. 572-0841. La Bocca Mia (M), Via Rocchi 36, tel. 572-3873. Vecchia Perusia (P), Via Rocchi 9, tel. 572-5900. La Fontanella di Porta Sole (P), Via delle Prome 2, tel. 573-4265.

Spello (p. 133).

Altitude 1,030 feet (344 meters). Population: 8,000. ZIP 06038. TAC 0742. I: Piazza Matteotti 3, tel. 301-009, fax 340-545.

SIGHTS.

Civic Picture Gallery (Pinacoteca Civica), Piazza Matteotti, tel. 301-497. Pinturicchio frescoes in Church of Santa Maria Maggiore. Consular Gate and Venus Gate. Roman amphitheater.

TO REACH SPELLO.

By road from Rome, 103 miles (165 kilometers) by Motorway A-1 to Orte, Superhighway Route 204 to Terni, Route 3 to Foligno, and Superhighway Route 75; from Florence, 116 miles (185 kilometers) by Motorway A-1 (south) to Valdichiana, Superhighway Route 75-bis to Perugia, and Superhighway Route 75. By rail from Rome in two hours via Foligno (change trains); from

Florence in about three hours via Terontola-Cortona (change of trains required at some times) and Perugia.

HOTELS.

Palazzo Bocci (T), Via Cavour 17, tel. 301-021, fax 301-464. La Bastiglia (M), Via dei Molini 16, tel. and fax 651-277. Del Teatro (M), Via Giulia 24, tel. 301-140, fax 301-612. Altavilla (M), Via Cavour, tel. 301-505, fax 651-258. Le Due Torri (P), Limiti di Spello (outskirts), tel. 651-249.

RESTAURANTS.

Il Molino (T), Piazza Matteotti 6-7, tel. 651-305. Il Frantoio (M), Via Consolare 16, tel. 301-134. Il Cacciatore (M), Via Giulia 42, tel. 651-141. Il Pinturicchio (M), Largo Mazzini 8, tel. 301-003.

Spoleto (p. 88).

Altitude 1,000–1,485 feet (305–453 meters). Population: 38,000. ZIP 06049. TAC 0743. I: Piazza della Libertà 7, tel. 220-311, fax 46-241. The Festival of Two Worlds, public relations office, Piazza del Duomo, tel. 40-369.

SIGHTS.

Cathedral with frescoes by Filippo Lippi. Civic Museum, Piazza della Signoria. City Hall with paintings by Lo Spagna, and Roman House, Piazza della Signoria, tel. 222-349. Fortress (La Rocca). Bridge of the Towers. Roman Theater. Arch of Drusus. Excursion to Monteluco with Convent of St. Francis and panorama (5 miles or 8 kilometers to the east, p. 102), and to Fountain of Clitumnus (7.5 miles or 12 kilometers to the north, p. 119).

TO REACH SPOLETO.

By road from Rome, 81 miles (130 kilometers) by Motorway A-1 to Orte, Superhighway Route 204 to Terni, and Route 3; from Florence, 136 miles (218 kilometers) by Motorway A-1 (south) to Valdichiana, Superhighway Route 75-bis to Perugia, Superhighway Route 75 (east) to Foligno, and Route 3 (south). By rail from Rome in one hour and twenty-five minutes. From Florence in about three hours via Orte (change trains) or in three to four hours via Terontola-Cortona (change of trains required at some times) and Foligno (change trains).

HOTELS.

Dei Duchi (T), Viale G. Matteotti 4, tel. 44-541, fax 44-543. Gattapone (T), Via del Ponte 6, tel. 223-447, fax 223-448. Il Barbarossa (T), Via Licina 12, tel. 43-644, fax 222-060. Nuovo Clitunno (M), Piazza Sordini 6, tel. 223-340, fax 222-663. Aurora (P), Via Apollinare 4, tel. 220-315, fax 221-885. Paradiso (P), near the summit of Monteluco, tel. 223-427, fax 223-082.

RESTAURANTS.

Il Tartufo (T), Via Garibaldi 24, tel. 40-236. Sabatini (T), Corso Mazzini 52-54, tel. 221-831. Locanda della Signoria (M), Piazza della Signoria 5 B, tel. 46-333.

Terni (p. 82).

Altitude 426 feet (130 meters). Population: 107,000. ZIP 05100. TAC 0744. I: Viale Cesare Battisti 7 A, tel. 423-048, fax 427-259.

SIGHTS.

Ruins of Roman amphitheater. Basilica of St. Valentine. Excursion to waterfalls of Le Marmore (p. 87).

TO REACH TERNI.

By road from Rome, 64 miles (103 kilometers) by Motorway A-1 to Orte and Superhighway Route 204; from Florence, 143 miles (229 kilometers) by Motorway A-1 (south) to Orte and Superhighway Route 204. By rail from Rome in one hour and ten to twenty minutes; from Florence in two hours and thirty minutes via Orte (change trains).

HOTELS.

Valentino (T), Via Plinio il Giovane 3, tel. 55-246, fax 55-240. Garden (M), Viale Bramante 4, tel. 300-041, fax 300-414.

RESTAURANTS.

Alfio (M), Via Galileo Galilei 4, tel. 420-120. Tacitus (M), Piazza Tacito 14, tel. 425-147.

Todi (p. 188).

Altitude 1,345 feet (410 meters). Population: 17,000. ZIP 06059. TAC 075. I: Piazza del Popolo 38, tel. 894-2526, fax 894-2406.

SIGHTS.

Piazza del Popolo with Cathedral and medieval palaces. Panorama from Piazza Garibaldi. Municipal Picture Gallery (Pinacoteca), Piazza del Popolo, tel. 894-561. Church of San Fortunato. Church of Santa Maria della Consolazione.

TO REACH TODI.

By road from Rome, 81 miles (130 kilometers) by Motorway A-1 to Orte, Superhighway Route 204 and Superhighway Route E-45; from Florence, 124 miles (199 kilometers) by Motorway A-1 (south) to Valdichiana, Superhighway Route 75-bis to Perugia, and Superhighway Route E-45 (south). By rail from Rome in two hours and thirty minutes to three hours via Terni (change to train of Ferrovia Centrale Umbra, FCU), and public bus over 2 miles (3.2 kilometers); from Florence in about 3.5 miles (5.6 kilometers) via Terontola-Cortona (change of trains required at some times) and Perugia-Ponte San Giovanni (change to FCU train), and bus, as above.

HOTELS.

Fonte Cesia (T), Via Lorenzo Leonj 3, tel. 894-3737, fax 894-4677. Bramante (M), Via Orvietana 48, tel. 894-8381, fax 894-8074. Villaluisa (M), Via Cortesi 147, tel. 894-8571, fax 894-8472. San Valentino (T), 2.5 miles (4 kilometers) southwest of Todi, tel. 894-4103, fax 894-8696. La Palazzetta (M), Località Asproli 23, 3 miles (5 kilometers) south of Todi, tel. 885-3219, fax 885-3358.

RESTAURANTS.

Umbria (M), Via San Bonaventura 13, tel. 894-2390. Jacopone-Da Peppino (M), Piazza Jacopone 5, tel. 894-2366. Lucaroni (M), Via Cortesi 5, tel. 894-2694. La Scaletta (P), Via della Scaletta, tel. 894-4422.

$\mathscr{T}$orgiano (p. 61).

Altitude 719 feet (219 meters). Population 5,000. ZIP 06089. TAC 075. I: Via Mazzini 21, 06100 Perugia, tel. (075) 572-5341, fax (075) 573-6828.

SIGHTS.

Panorama with vineyards. Wine Museum, Corso Vittorio Emanuele 1, tel. 988-0200.

TO REACH TORGIANO.

By road from Rome, 99 miles (158 kilometers) by Motorway A-1 to Orte, Superhighway Route 204, Superhighway Route E-45 to Ponte Nuovo, and provincial highway (east) for 2 miles (3.2 kilometers); from Florence, 114 miles (183 kilometers) by Motorway A-1 (south) to Valdichiana, Superhighway Route 75-bis to Perugia, Superhighway Route E-45 (south) to Sant'Andrea d'Aglio, and provincial highway (east) over 3.7 miles (6 kilometers). By rail from Rome, two hours and fifty minutes to Perugia via Foligno (change of trains required at most times), proceeding by public bus over 10 miles (16 kilometers); from Florence in two hours and thirty minutes via Terontola-Cortona (change of trains required at some times) to Perugia, proceeding by bus, as above.

HOTEL AND RESTAURANT.

Le Tre Vaselle (T), tel. 988-0447, fax 988-0214.

$\mathcal{T}revi$ (p. 123).

Altitude 1,352 feet (412 meters). Population 7,500. ZIP 06039. TAC 0742. I: Piazza Garibaldi 12, 06034 Foligno, tel. (0742) 350-493, fax (0742) 340-545.

SIGHTS.

Town Hall with Picture Gallery (Pinacoteca). Town walls. Church of St. Mary of the Tears. Panorama of terraced olive groves.

TO REACH TREVI.

By road from Rome, 94 miles (150 kilometers) by Motorway A-1 to Orte, Superhighway Route 204 to Terni, and Route 3; from Florence, 126 miles (202 kilometers) by Motorway A-1 (south) to Valdichiana, Superhighway Route 75-bis to Perugia, Superhighway Route 75 (east) to Foligno, and Route 3 (south). By rail from Rome in one hour and forty-five minutes; from Florence in about three hours via Terontola Cortona (change of trains required at some times) and Foligno (change trains).

HOTEL.

Pian di Zucchero (P), Via Camporeale 5, tel. 781-390.

RESTAURANTS.

L'Ulivo (M), Via Monte Bianco 23, on northern outskirts, two miles (3.2 kilometers) from town center, tel. 78-969. La Taverna del Pescatore (M), Via Camporeale 3, tel. 780-920.

Tuoro del Trasimeno (p. 32).

Altitude 1,014 feet (309 meters). Population: 3,500. ZIP 06069. TAC 075. I: Piazza Mazzini 10, 06061, Castiglione del Lago, tel.. (075) 965-2484, fax (075) 965-2763.

SIGHTS.

Battlefields of Hannibal's 217 B.C. victory. Campo del Sole with modern sculptures.

TO REACH TUORO.

By road from Rome, 128 miles (205 kilometers) by Motorway A-1 to Chiusi-Chianciano Terme, Route 71 to Borghetto, and Superhighway Route 75-bis; from Florence, 81 miles (130 kilometers) by Motorway A-1 (south) to Valdichiana and Superhighway Route 75-bis. By rail from Rome, two hours to two hours and twenty minutes via Terontola-Cortona (change trains); from Florence, in about two hours via Terontola-Cortona (change of trains required at some times.)

HOTEL.

Volante Inn (M), Via Sette Mártiri 52, tel. 826-107, fax 825-088.

RESTAURANT.

Paradiso del Vecchio Mulino, tel. 826-185.

Umbértide (p. 65)

Altitude 810 feet (247 meters). Population: 14,000. ZIP 06019. TAC 075. I: Via Raffaele da Cesare 2 B, 06012, Città di Castello, tel. (075) 855-4817, fax (075) 855-2100.

SIGHTS.

Fortress. Church of Santa Maria della Reggia. Church of Santa Croce with Luca Signorelli altarpiece. Excursion to Civitella Ranieri Castle (p. 66), 3 miles (5 kilometers) east of Umbértide.

TO REACH UMBÉRTIDE.

By road from Rome, 131 miles (209 kilometers) by Motorway A-1 to Orte, Superhighway Route 204, and Superhighway Route E-45; from Florence, 104 miles (167 kilometers) by Motorway A-1 (south) to Arezzo, Route 73 to Sansepolcro, and Super-highway E-45 (south). By rail from Rome, three hours and thirty minutes via Terni, proceeding by Ferrovia Centrale Umbra (FCU) local train; from Florence, in one hour and fifty minutes to Arezzo, proceeding by public bus to Città di Castello to continue either by FCU train or public bus.

HOTEL AND RESTAURANT.

Rio (M), Strada Statale (Route 3-bis), 2 miles (3.2 kilometers) southeast of Umbértide, tel. (075) 941-5033, fax (075) 941-7029.